THE UNIVERSITY OF CHICAGO SCHOOL MATHEMATICS PROJECT

Everyday Mathematics

D1245809

Journal II

Everyday Learning Corporation

Evanston, Illinois

On the Cover: American, Mount Holly, New Jersey, Ella Marie Deacon Quilt,
              needlework; quilt cotton, 1842, 265.7 cm × 274.3 cm, Gift of Mrs. Betsey
              Leeds Tait Pater, 1978.923. Photograph by Nancy Finn.
              © 1990 The Art Institute of Chicago, All Rights Reserved.

ISBN 1-57039-060-6

23456789HS9998979695

Contents

Unit 9: Percents

Unit 10: Mammals: An Investigation

Unit 11: Perimeter and Area

Unit 12: Rates

Unit 13: Three-Dimensional Shapes and Volume

Activity Sheets

Reading Big Numbers

trillions			billions			millions			thousands			ones		
100	10	1	100	10	1	100	10	1	100	10	1	100	10	1
9	2	1	9	4	3	7	0	5	0	2	9	4	0	0

Very big numbers can be scary. But they don't need to be. Look for the commas that separate groups of 3 digits. They will help you identify the thousands, millions, billions, and so on. Or think this way:

Digits followed by **3** whole-number places name **thousands**.
Digits followed by **6** whole-number places name **millions**.
Digits followed by **9** whole-number places name **billions**.
Digits followed by **12** whole-number places name **trillions**.

Numbers in trillions are about as big as you see in newspapers (perhaps to name the United States budget), but for really big numbers, there are also:

quadrillions—digits followed by **15** whole-number places,
quintillions—digits followed by **18** whole-number places,
sextillions—digits followed by **21** whole-number places,

and **septillions**, **octillions**, and beyond.

Each group of 3 places has a value 1000 times greater than the value of the places in the group to its right. For example:

1 million is the same as 1000 thousands.
1 billion is the same as 1000 millions.
1 trillion is the same as 1000 billions.

Look at the place-value chart at the top of the page. The number in the chart is read as 921 trillion, 943 billion, 705 million, 29 thousand, 4 hundred.

 ## Other Names for Big Numbers

Prefixes such as **kilo-** and **mega-** are often used to name large numbers of things. For example, a kilometer is a thousand meters. The prefix **giga-** is used to name a billion and **tera-** to name a trillion things.

These prefixes come from the Greek language. Mega- comes from the word for large, giga- from the word for giant, and tera- from the word for monster.

Use with Lesson 66.

A 40-by-50 Array

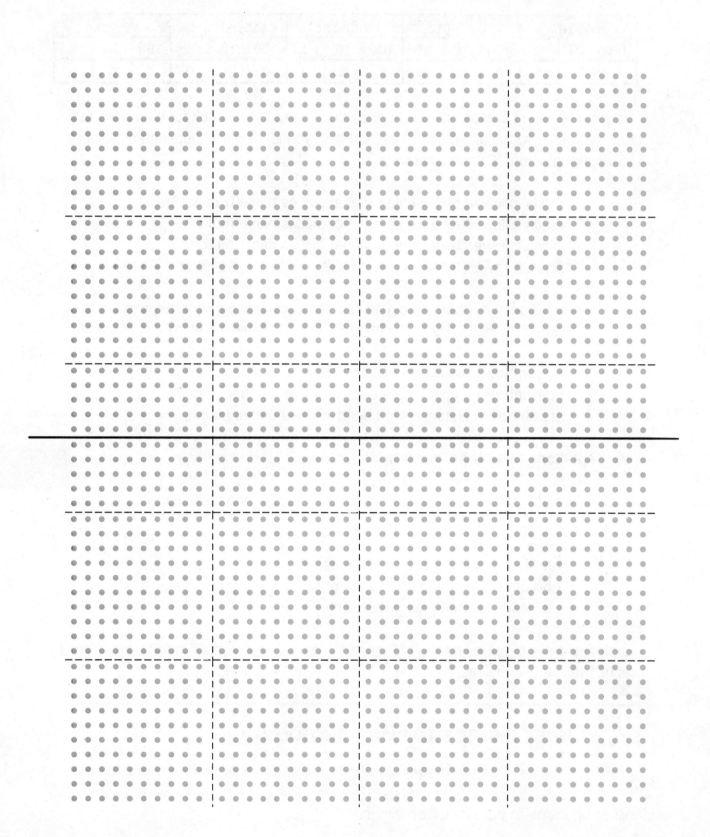

How Much is a Billion?

1. How many dots are on page 146? _____ dots

2. How many dots would be on:

    a. 5 such pages? _____ dots

    b. 50 pages? _____ dots

    c. 500 pages? _____ dots

3. Copier paper comes in packages of 500 sheets. A package of 500 sheets is called a ream. How many dots would be on the paper in:

    a. 1 ream? (Hint: Look at Problem 2.) _____ dots

    b. 10 reams? (1 carton) _____ dots

    c. 100 reams? (10 cartons) _____ dots

    d. 1000 reams? (100 cartons) _____ dots

 ## To Touch the Stars

The nearest star other than our Sun is *Proxima Centauri*, which is about 25 trillion miles away. That's 2.5×10^{13} miles. Even traveling at 100,000 miles per second, it would still take almost 8 years to reach it.

Source: *The Guinness Book of Records, 1993*. New York: Facts on File, 1992.

Use with Lesson 66.

Math Boxes

---

1. Give the value of the bold digit in each numeral.

    a.   12,783,**8**83   _____

    b.   **5**00,911   _____

    c.   19,023,**9**84   _____

    d.   167,0**2**7,338   _____

---

2. Solve.

    $5 * 7 =$ _____

    $50 * 7 =$ _____

    $5 * 700 =$ _____

    $350 \div 7 =$ _____

  $70 + 70 + 70 + 70 + 70 = 5 *$ _____

3. Name three fractions equivalent to $\frac{1}{6}$.

     _____

     _____

     _____

---

4. Fill in the missing values on the number line below.

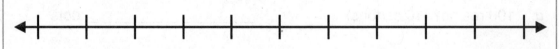

2.6   *2.67*   2.7

    ____   ____   ____   ____   ____   ____   ____   ____

Place Value and Powers of 10

	Millions	Hundred Thousands	Ten Thousands	Thousands	Hundreds	Tens	Ones
A					100		1
B	10 [100,000's]			10 [100's]			10 [tenths]
C			10 * 10 * 10 * 10		10 * 10		
D		10^5		10^3			10^0

1. Write the standard place names in Row A in the place-value chart above.

2. Fill in the missing information in Row B to show that the value of each place is 10 times as much as the value of the place to its right.

3. In Row C, write the place names as products of tens.

4. In Row D, use exponents to write the place names as powers of 10. The exponent shows how many times 10 is used as a factor. It also shows how many zeros are in the standard place name.

Math Boxes

1. Use your protractor to make angles with the following measures.

   a. 15°   b. 170°

2. Write and solve a subtraction number story using 3460 and 5238.

   _____

   _____

   _____

   _____

   _____

   Answer: _____

3. Sara had collected 30 leaves to share with her 6 friends equally. On the way to school she lost 2 of them. When she arrived at school she shared them with her 6 friends. How many leaves did each child receive?

   _____

4. Round the following numbers to the nearest thousand.

   a. 8,289,500 _____

   b. 725,311 _____

   c. 451,062 _____

   d. 12,000,852 _____

Use with Lesson 67.

The U.S. Census

A **census** is a survey taken by the government of a country. The government collects information about the people who live there. It counts the population and asks questions about people's education, occupation, income, languages spoken, and much more. This information is used in planning what services to provide.

The United States was the first nation in history to require a census. This requirement is written in the U.S. Constitution. By law, a census must be taken every 10 years. The first U.S. Census took place in 1790.

The population count is used to determine how many representatives each state will have in the U.S. House of Representatives. According to the latest census, the U.S. population in 1990 was 248,709,873.

For many years, census information was collected through personal interviews and recorded on special census forms. Since 1960, most of these forms have been sent out by mail. People then fill out the forms and mail them back to the Census Bureau. However, not all people can be reached by mail. For example, homeless people have no address. People who live in remote locations or who live in the country illegally are often difficult to find.

For the 1990 census, the Census Bureau employed 300,000 persons, called **enumerators**, to help collect census information from people who were difficult to reach or who did not return the completed forms. Even with their help, not everyone was counted. The Bureau estimates that over 3 million people were missed in the 1990 census.

Once the information has been collected, the Census Bureau must analyze the data and publish the results. This is a huge job. The results of the 1880 census took over 7 years to publish. For the 1890 census, the inventor Herman Hollerith developed a machine that speeded up the tabulation of the results. Using Hollerith's machine, it took less than 3 years to tabulate the 1890 census data, saving 5 million dollars.

Hollerith's machine was an early computer. Information was recorded by punching holes in cards, called punch cards. The cards were then fed into the machine, which would sort the data on the cards.

What device is used to enter data in modern computers?

Use with Lesson 68.

Rounding Numbers

To round a number to a given place:

1. Find the digit in the place you are rounding to.

2. Rewrite the number, replacing all digits to the right of this digit with zeros. This is the **lower number**.

3. Add 1 to the digit in the place you are rounding to. This is the **higher number**.

4. Find the number halfway between the lower number and the higher number.

5. Ask yourself: "Is the number I am rounding closer to the lower number or to the higher number?"

6. Round to the closer of the two numbers.

Example 1: Round 7385 to the nearest thousand.

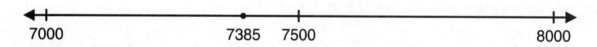

7385 is closer to 7000 than to 8000. Therefore, 7385, rounded to the nearest thousand, is 7000.

Example 2: Round 7385 to the nearest hundred.

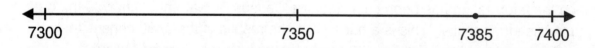

7385 is closer to 7400 than to 7300. Therefore, 7385, rounded to the nearest hundred, is 7400.

Example 3: Round 7385 to the nearest ten.

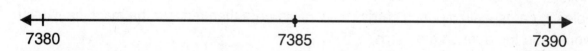

7385 is halfway between 7380 and 7390. We usually round halfway numbers to the higher number. Therefore, 7385, rounded to the nearest ten, is 7390.

Date _____ Time _____

Rounding Practice

In each of Problems 1–3, locate the lower number, the higher number, the halfway number, and the number being rounded on the number line.

1. Round 73,546 to the nearest hundred.

_____   _____   _____

    73,546, rounded to the nearest hundred, is _____ .

2. Round 73,546 to the nearest ten.

_____   _____   _____

    73,546, rounded to the nearest ten, is _____ .

3. Round 73,546 to the nearest thousand.

_____   _____   _____

    73,546, rounded to the nearest thousand, is _____ .

4. Round 42,375,218 to the nearest million.   _____

5. Round 58,083 to the nearest hundred.   _____

6. Round 6,792,044 to the nearest ten thousand.   _____

7. Round 31,888 to the nearest ten.   _____

8. Round 30,499,621 to the nearest hundred thousand.   _____

9. Round 30,499,621 to the nearest thousand.   _____

Use with Lesson 68.

Geographical Measurements

Have you ever wondered how the heights of mountains, the depths of oceans, or the lengths of rivers are measured? How accurate are these measurements?

Vertical measurements, such as heights and depths, are given as distances above or below sea level. The level of a sea or ocean is not exactly the same at all times— it may vary, depending on the tides, the gravitational force of the moon, and other factors. The same sea level is used in all parts of the world.

Many measurements are made with the help of surveying instruments. These measurements can be made more accurate by using data collected with the help of satellites.

- Because every part of a city is not the same height above sea level, cities in the United States have a marker located somewhere in the downtown area. The elevation of the city is the height of the marker above sea level and is accurate to the nearest foot.

- The height of a mountain pass is its elevation at its highest point. Measurements are usually made on both sides of the pass. Because the landscape may be rugged, the reported heights of mountain passes may be less accurate than the elevations of cities.

- The depth of various points in an ocean is measured by sending sound signals to the ocean floor. The time it takes for these signals to reach bottom and bounce back is used to determine the depth. Other factors, such as water temperature, must also be taken into account. Depth measurements are usually accurate to the nearest 10 feet.

Other measurements are made without measuring the object itself.

- The length of a river is usually measured using very accurate maps, created with the help of satellite photography. An instrument the size of a ballpoint pen, but with a very small wheel instead of a ball at its tip, is moved steadily on the map along the full length of the river. Using the map scale, the number of times the wheel rotates is converted into the actual length of the river. Because the tracing on the map is made on a flat surface, this measurement must be corrected to take into account the fact that the river does not flow on a level surface. Length-of-river measurements are usually accurate to the nearest mile for each 1000 miles of river. For example, the length of a 3000-mile long river is probably accurate to the nearest 3 miles.

Use with Lesson 69.

Choosing the Next World Tour Destination

It is time to leave Europe and fly to Region 3—the continent of South America. Before you and your classmates decide which country to visit next, you will collect information about the countries in Region 3. Then you can vote on which city to fly to. Use your *World Tour Book* to answer the following questions.

1. Which country in Region 3 has:

   a. The largest population? _____

   b. The smallest population? _____

   c. The largest area? _____

   d. The smallest area? _____

2. Which capital has:

   a. The largest population? _____

   b. The smallest population? _____

3. At this time of year, which capital has:

   a. The warmest weather? _____

   b. The coolest weather? _____

   c. The greatest amount of rain? _____

   d. The least amount of rain? _____

4. Which country has:

   a. The greatest percent of population ages 0–14? _____

   b. The smallest percent of population that age? _____

Use with Lesson 69.

Choosing the Next World Tour Destination (continued)

5. Which country has:

a. The largest percent of urban population
(people who live in towns and cities)? _____

b. The largest percent of rural population
(people who live in the country)? _____

6. Which city in South America has the largest population? _____

Is it the capital of a country? _____

7. Choose the capital of a country in Region 3 you would like to visit first. Use the
facts you have found in your *World Tour Book* and any other information you
may know to help you make your choice. Do you know someone who has lived
there or gone there for a visit? Have you read any books or stories about South
America? What do you know about plant and animal life? About the customs of
the people? Do you know any words in Spanish or Portuguese?

I would like to visit _____ because _____

_____

_____

_____

_____

_____

_____

Representing Population Counts with Dot Paper

Dot Paper Information
Each sheet of paper has 2000 dots on it. A ream has 500 sheets. A carton contains 10 reams.

Pretend that each dot on a sheet of paper stands for 1 person.

1. How many persons are represented by 1 ream of dot paper?   _____

2. How many persons are represented by 1 full carton of paper?   _____

3. How many full cartons and about how many extra reams of dot paper are needed to represent the population of each South American country in the table? (There will be some leftover paper, but you don't need to count it.)

Country	Population	Number of full cartons	Number of extra reams
Argentina	32,901,000		
Bolivia	7,323,000		
Brazil	158,000,000		
Chile	13,528,000		
Colombia	35,000,000		
Ecuador	10,933,000		
Paraguay	4,929,000		
Peru	22,767,000		
Uruguay	3,139,000		
Venezuela	20,675,000		

4. The population of Brazil is about 5 times the population of which country in the table?   _____

5. True or false? The population of Brazil is about $\frac{1}{2}$ the total population of all the countries in the table.   _____

Use with Lesson 70.

Math Boxes

1. The square below represents $\frac{1}{4}$. Draw one whole or $\frac{4}{4}$ on the grid at the right.

2. Solve.

   45 / 9 = _____

   450 / 90 = _____

   9 * _____ = 450

   _____ = 90 + 90 + 90 + 90 + 90

3. Books are packed 9 to a box. How many boxes do you need to pack 45 books?

   _____

4. Tina is facing north. She turns 45° clockwise, 90° counterclockwise, and 135° counterclockwise. What direction is she facing now?

   _____

Date _____ Time _____

Math Message

Imagine that the airline you are using on the World Tour will give you a $50 discount coupon for every 5000 miles you fly. Suppose you have flown the distances shown in the table at the right.

How many coupons would
you have earned so far? _____

St. Paul	⇒	Washington	820 miles
Washington	⇒	Cairo	5980
Cairo	⇒	Accra	2420
Accra	⇒	Cairo	2420
Cairo	⇒	Budapest	1380
Budapest	⇒	London	1040
London	⇒	Budapest	1040
Budapest	⇒	Brasilia	5650

Planning a Driving Trip

Pretend that you and your partner are planning to travel from your hometown to one of the cities shown on the map on the next page. If your hometown is not on the map, plan to drive to the nearest city on the map first. Your teacher will give you the distance and driving time from your hometown to this city. Your route should take you through at least four cities on the map.

You plan to drive about 8 hours a day and then stop for the night. You want to find out how many **days** it will take you to reach your destination.

1. Record your route, driving times, and driving distances in the table below.

From-To	Driving Time	Driving Distance

2. How many hours in all will you have to drive?   about _____ hours

3. How many days will it take to complete the trip?   _____ days

4. How many miles in all will you drive?   about _____ miles

Use with Lesson 71.

Estimated U.S. Distances and Driving Times

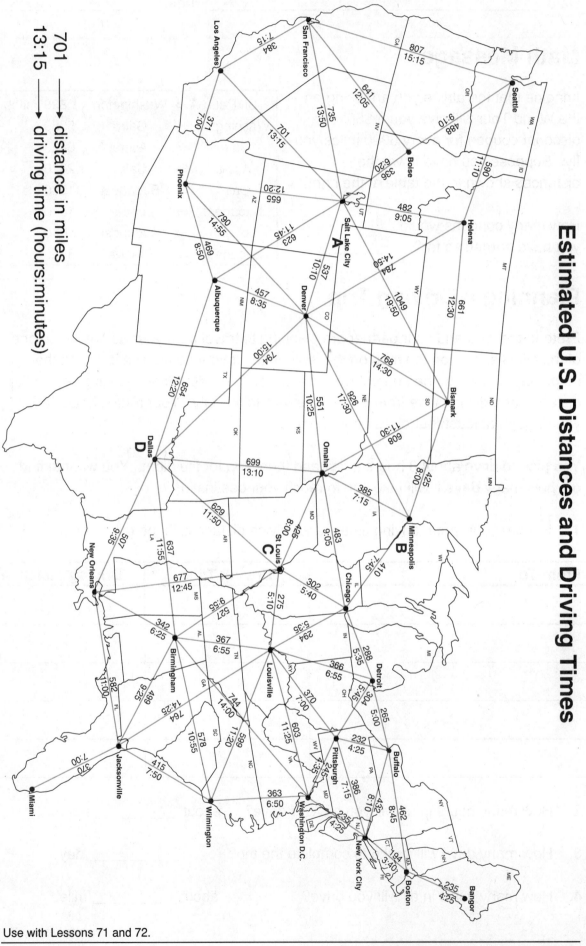

701 $\longrightarrow$ distance in miles

13:15 $\longrightarrow$ driving time (hours:minutes)

Math Message

Pretend you are driving from Miami to Jacksonville, Florida, then to Birmingham, Alabama, and last to Louisville, Kentucky. Find the **exact** total driving distance and driving time, using the information on the map on page 160.

Then ask your partner to check your answers, using a calculator.

1. Total driving distance: _____ miles

2. Total driving time: _____ hours _____ minutes

A Traveling Salesperson Problem—An Unsolved Problem in Mathematics and Computer Science

A traveling salesperson plans to visit several cities. To save time and money, the salesperson wants the trip to be as short as possible.   If the salesperson is only going to a few cities, it will be fairly easy to figure out the shortest possible route. But what if the salesperson travels to 10 cities? There would be 3,628,800 possible routes. Even with a computer it is difficult to figure out the shortest route!

Computers are often used to solve mathematical problems. They are especially useful when a problem involves millions or billions of calculations. Computers, however, can't solve everything. If the salesperson needs to visit 100 cities, there is no computer that has enough power or memory to examine all the possible routes. (There are more possible routes than atoms on the Earth.) Computer scientists are still trying to find methods to solve this problem, without having to do an impossible number of calculations.

Try to think like a computer. Pick four cities on the map on page 160. Find the shortest route that would take you from one city to each of the other three. Remember, computers do not try out every route to find the shortest one. Computer scientists design programs that tell the computer to estimate some routes and ignore any that do not make sense.

Use with Lesson 72.

Math Boxes

---

1. Complete.

   a. 156 minutes is the same as

      ____ hours and ____ minutes.

   b. 157 hours is the same as

      ____ days and ____ hours.

   c. 58 months is the same as

      ____ years and ____ months.

---

2. During a recent survey at Martin Elementary, the results showed that out of the 800 students surveyed, about $\frac{3}{4}$ of them said they liked pizza as their favorite food. How many students of the 800 liked pizza as their favorite food?

about _____

---

3. Complete the following.

   a. $80 * \underline{\hspace{1cm}} = 160$

   b. $1600 = 20 * \underline{\hspace{1cm}}$

   c. $200 = 1600 / \underline{\hspace{1cm}}$

   d. $800 = 1600 / \underline{\hspace{1cm}}$

   e. $16{,}000 = \underline{\hspace{1cm}} * 200$

---

4. Make up a set of 7 numbers that have the following landmarks:

mode: 21

median: 24

maximum: 35

range: 20

_____ _____ _____ _____

_____ _____ _____

---

5. **a.** What time is the clock showing?
(Answer to the nearest minute.)

      _____ : _____

   b. About what time will it be in 40 minutes?

      _____ : _____

   c. About what time will it be in 78 minutes?

      _____ : _____

Date _____ Time _____

Math Message

Answer the following questions as best as you can.

1. How many glasses of fruit juice did you drink in the last 7 days? _____

2. How many candy bars did you eat in the last 7 days? _____

3. How many hot dogs did you eat in the last 7 days? _____

4. How many hamburgers did you eat in the last 7 days? _____

 ## What Do Americans Eat?

According to a 1984 survey by the U.S. Department of Agriculture, the "average" American eats about 1431 pounds of food per year. This is about 4 pounds per day.

This survey and others found that in one year, the "average" American eats or drinks about:

2	pounds of broccoli
4	pounds of potato chips
7	pounds of peanuts
11	gallons of fruit juice
18	pounds of candy
27	pounds of lettuce
44	gallons of soft drinks
47	gallons of water
80	hot dogs
89	pounds of fresh fruit
121	pounds of potatoes
200	hamburgers
255	eggs

Source: Biracree, Tom and Nancy Biracree. *Almanac of the American People.* New York: Facts on File, 1988.

Use with Lesson 73.

More Averages

For each problem, estimate whether the answer is in the tens, hundreds, thousands, or more. Circle the appropriate box.

1.   An average of about 23 new species of insects are discovered each day. About how many new species are discovered in one year?

10's	100's	1000's	10,000's	100,000's	millions

2.   A housefly beats its wings about 190 times per second. That's about how many times per minute?

10's	100's	1000's	10,000's	100,000's	millions

3.   A blue whale weighs about as much as 425,000 kittens. About how many kittens weigh as much as 4 blue whales?

10's	100's	1000's	10,000's	100,000's	millions

4.   An average bee can lift about 300 times its own weight.   If a 170-pound person were as strong as a bee, about how many pounds could this person lift?

10's	100's	1000's	10,000's	100,000's	millions

Challenge

5.   Elephants spend an average of 16 hours a day eating. An average African elephant lives about 35 years. About how many hours does an elephant spend eating in a lifetime?

10's	100's	1000's	10,000's	100,000's	millions

Use with Lesson 73.

Date _____ Time _____

Math Boxes

1. Name something in your room that is:

   about 1 cm long   _____

   about 10 cm long   _____

   about 50 cm long   _____

2. Draw a quadrangle that is both a rhombus and a rectangle.

   What is it called? _____

3. How many line
   segments shown
   below can you name? _____

       A   B   C   D

   Write their names.

   _____

   _____

4. Solve.

   7 * _____ = 21

   40 ÷ _____ = 5

   _____ ÷ 7 = 6

   _____ * 10 = 120

   9 * 7 = _____

Use with Lesson 73.

The Partial-Products Algorithm

1. Multiply. Show your work in the grid below.

   Example:
   6 * 463 = ?

   a. _____ = 3 * 470   b. 234 * 4 = _____

   c. 2 * 1523 = _____

   ```
     4 6 3
   *     6
   2 4 0 0   ← 6 [400's]
     3 6 0   ← 6 [60's]
   +   1 8   ← 6 [3's]
   2 7 7 8
   ```

2. On an "average" day, about 217 pairs of twins are born in the U.S. About how many children, who are twins, are born in 1 week?

   a. Is the answer in the:

10's	100's	1000's	10,000's	100,000's	millions

   b. Calculate the answer in the space below.   about _____ children

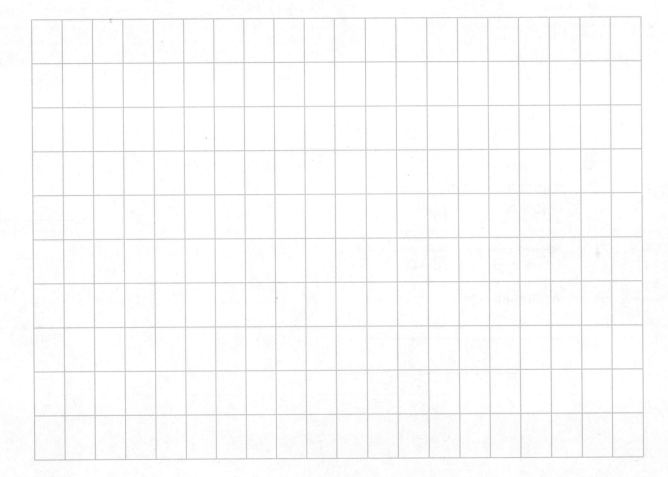

Math Boxes

1. Round the following numbers to the nearest thousand.

   a. 36,892 _____

   b. 3245 _____

   c. 92,567 _____

   d. 105,833 _____

2. Put these numbers in order from smallest to largest.

   0.6   0.06   0.43   0.9

   _____ _____ _____ _____

3. When you roll a regular die, what fraction of the time can you expect to get either a 1 or a 6?

   _____

4. Complete.

   7 weeks = _____ days

   4 weeks 3 days = _____ days

   4 m = _____ cm

   3 cm = _____ mm

   200 cm = _____ m

5. Find the input numbers.

   Rule : − 9

in	out
_____	10
_____	1
_____	99
_____	1059

6. For the set of numbers

   8, 20, 17, 16, 5, 15, 9

   what is the:

   maximum? _____

   minimum? _____

   range? _____

Number Stories

For each problem, estimate whether the answer is in the tens, hundreds, thousands, or more. Circle the appropriate box.

1. A test found that a light bulb lasts an average of 63 days after being turned on. About how many hours is that?

10's	100's	1000's	10,000's	100,000's	millions

2. Eighteen newborn hummingbirds weigh about 1 ounce. About how many of them does it take to make 1 pound? (1 pound = 16 ounces)

10's	100's	1000's	10,000's	100,000's	millions

3. The average person drinks about 15 glasses of milk a month. About how many glasses of milk is that per year?

10's	100's	1000's	10,000's	100,000's	millions

4. A full-grown oak tree loses an average of about 7 tons of water through its leaves per day. That's about how many tons per year?

10's	100's	1000's	10,000's	100,000's	millions

Challenge

5. The famous painter, Picasso, painted an average of 5 pictures a week for 75 years. About how many pictures did he paint in his lifetime?

10's	100's	1000's	10,000's	100,000's	millions

Use with Lesson 75.

Date _____ Time _____

Number Stories (continued)

6. Carry out the multiplications for each problem. Show your work on the
    computation grid below. Write your answer next to the problems on page 168.

Use with Lesson 75.

Math Message

Suppose you filled your classroom from floor to ceiling with dot paper.

1. About how many dots do you think there would be on all the paper needed to fill your classroom? Make a check mark next to your guess.

    _____ Less than a million

    _____ Between a million and half a billion

    _____ Between half a billion and a billion

    _____ More than a billion

2. One ream of paper weighs about 5 pounds. About how many pounds would the paper needed to fill the room weigh? Make a check mark next to your guess.

    _____ Less than 100,000 pounds

    _____ Between 100,000 and 500,000 pounds

    _____ Between 500,000 pounds and a million pounds

    _____ More than a million pounds

Work with your classmates to make more accurate estimates of the number of dots and the weight of the dot paper needed to fill your classroom. Tell what you did.

My group's estimates:

Number of dots: _____   Weight of paper: _____

_____

_____

_____

_____

_____

Use with Lesson 76.

Math Boxes

---

1. I am a number. If you double me and add 6, you get 40.

   Who am I? _____

2. Zena earned $12. She spent $9.

   What fraction of her earnings did she spend? _____

   What fraction did she have left? _____

3. Sketch an angle that is greater than 90°, but less than 180°. Estimate the measure of the angle that you have drawn.

   about _____ °

5. Solve.

   a. $7 * 208 =$ _____

   b. $26 * 18 =$ _____

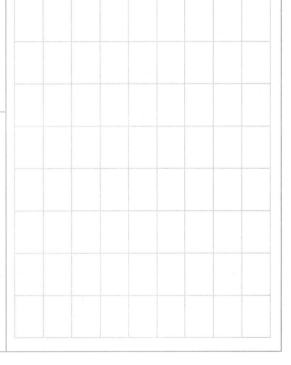

4. Draw a set of 12 balloons. Circle $\frac{5}{12}$ of the set. Put an X over $\frac{1}{4}$ of the set.

Use with Lesson 76.

A Multiplication-Wrestling Competition

1. Twelve players entered a multiplication-wrestling competition.
   The numbers they chose are shown in the following table.
   Their score is the product of the numbers they chose. For
   example, Aidan's score is 741, because 31 $*$ 57 = 741. Which
   of the 12 players do you think has the highest score? _____

Group A	Group B	Group C
Aidan: 13 $*$ 57	Indira: 15 $*$ 73	Miguel: 17 $*$ 35
Colette: 13 $*$ 75	Jelani: 15 $*$ 37	Rex: 17 $*$ 53
Emily: 31 $*$ 75	Kuniko: 51 $*$ 37	Sarah: 71 $*$ 53
Gunnar: 31 $*$ 57	Liza: 51 $*$ 73	Tanisha: 71 $*$ 35

To check your guess, do the following.

2. In each pair, cross out the one with the lower score.

Aidan; Colette	Indira; Jelani	Miguel; Rex
Emily; Gunnar	Kuniko; Liza	Sarah; Tanisha

   Then cross out the names of the players with the lower scores in the table in
   Part 1.

3. Two players are left in Group A. Cross out the name of the one with the
   lower score.

   Two players are left in Group B. Cross out the name of the one with the
   lower score.

   Two players are left in Group C. Cross out the name of the one with the
   lower score.

   Which 3 players are still left?

   _____

4. Of the 3 players who are left, which player has the lowest score?

   _____   Cross out that player's name.

5. There are 2 players left. What are their scores? _____

6. Who won the competition? _____

Basic Use of a Transparent Mirror

A labeled picture of a transparent mirror is shown at the right.

Notice that the mirror has a **recessed** edge, used for drawing lines. Some transparent mirrors have a drawing edge both on the top and on the bottom.

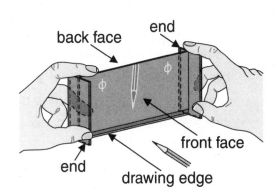

back face   end

front face

end   drawing edge

Place your transparent mirror on this page so that its drawing edge lies along line K. Look through the transparent mirror to read the "backward" message below.

_____

K

(The following message is printed backward, to be read through the transparent mirror:)

If you have followed the directions correctly, you are now able to read this message. Here are a few things to remember when using your transparent mirror.

• Always look into the front face of the transparent mirror. In this position, the drawing edge will be facing you.

• Use your transparent mirror on flat surfaces like your desk or a table top.

• Use a sharp pencil when tracing along the drawing edge.

• Experiment and have fun!

Use with Lesson 78.

Date _____ Time _____

Math Boxes

1. After school Sally spent $\frac{3}{4}$ of an hour watching TV and $\frac{1}{2}$ of an hour drawing. How many minutes did she spend on her after-school activities?

   _____

2. Using your ruler draw a line segment that is 2 inches long. Locate and mark the following inch-measurements on the line segment: $\frac{3}{4}$, $\frac{7}{8}$, $1\frac{1}{8}$, and $1\frac{1}{2}$.

3. Solve.

   a. 23 * 52 = _____

   b. 98 * 46 = _____

   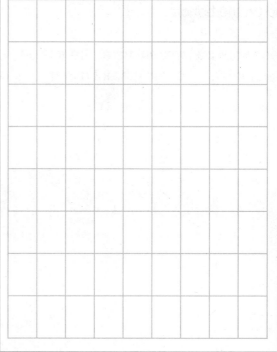

4. Fill in the missing numbers on the number lines.

   a.

   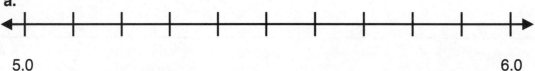

   5.0   6.0

   b.

   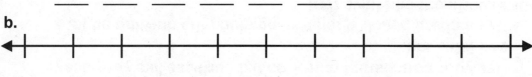

   4.73   5.43   5.73

Dart Game

Tear out Activity Sheet 12 from the back of your journal.

Practice before you play the game on the front of the Activity Sheet. One partner chooses dart A and the other partner dart B. Try to hit the target with your own dart, using the transparent mirror. **Do not practice with your partner's dart.**

Now, play the game with your partner.

Directions: Take turns. When it is your turn, use the other dart, the one you did not use for practice. Try to hit the target by placing the transparent mirror on the page, but **do not look through the mirror.** Then both you and your partner look through the mirror to see where the dart hit the target. Keep score.

Pocket-Billiard Game

Practice before you play the game on the back of Activity Sheet 12. Choose a ball (1, 2, 3, or 4) and a pocket (A, B, C, D, E, or F). Try to get the ball into the pocket, using the transparent mirror.

Now play the game.

Directions: Take turns. When it is your turn, say which ball and which pocket you picked: for example, "Ball 2 to go into pocket D." Try to get the ball into the pocket by placing the transparent mirror on the billiard table, but **do not look through the mirror.** Then both you and your partner look through the mirror to check whether the ball went into the pocket. Devise a scoring system with your partner.

Challenge
By using a ruler, you can find exactly where to put the mirror so that the ball will go into the pocket. Try it. For example, exactly where would you put the mirror so that ball 2 will go into pocket D? Check your answer with the mirror.

Try your method with many different combinations of balls and pockets.

Math Boxes

1. a. Write a fraction and decimal for the shaded part of the square.

$\frac{3}{5} = \dfrac{\boxed{}}{10} = 0.\underline{\hspace{1.5cm}}$

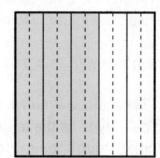

b. How many tenths? _____

2. a. Shade $\frac{5}{6}$ of the hexagon.

b. Shade $\frac{2}{3}$ of the hexagon.

3. A number has

   3 tens

   8 hundred thousands

   0 ones

   2 millions

   9 thousands

   4 hundreds

   7 ten thousands

Write the number. _____

4. Solve. Use your tape measure if you need help.

a. 10 cm = _____ mm

b. 3.6 m = _____ cm

c. 560 cm = _____ m

d. 82 mm = _____ cm

5. Write 5 other names for $\frac{1}{4}$.

a. _____

b. _____

c. _____

d. _____

e. _____

Math Boxes

---

1. **367.53**

Add the following to the number above:

6 tens, 4 hundredths, and 2 tenths. What is the new number?

_____

2. Mary has 27 pictures. She gives $\frac{1}{3}$ of them to her sister Barb and $\frac{2}{3}$ to her cousin Sara.

   a. How many pictures does Barb get? _____

   b. How many pictures does Sara get? _____

   c. How many does Mary keep for herself? _____

3. Solve.

   a. 14 * 8 = _____

   b. 18 * 39 = _____

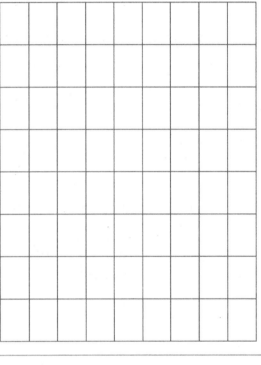

5. Shade more than $\frac{1}{2}$ but less than $\frac{3}{4}$ of the square.

Write the value as a decimal and fraction.

Fraction: _____

Decimal: _____

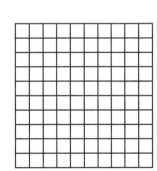

Date _____ Time _____

Line Symmetry

Tear out Activity Sheets 14, 15, 16, and 17 from the back of your journal.

1. The drawings on Activity Sheet 14 show only half-pictures. Figure out what each whole picture shows. Then use the transparent mirror to complete each picture. Use the recessed side of the edge of the mirror to draw the mirror line.

2. The pictures on Activity Sheet 15 are symmetric.

    a. Use the transparent mirror to draw the line of symmetry for the bat and the turtle.

    b. Cut out the other three pictures and find their lines of symmetry by folding.

    c. Which picture has two lines of symmetry? _____

3. Cut out each of the polygons on Activity Sheets 16 and 17. Find all the lines of symmetry for each polygon. Record the results in the table below.

Polygon	Number of lines of symmetry		Polygon	Number of lines of symmetry
A			F	
B			G	
C			H	
D			I	
E			J	

4. Study the results in the table. How many lines of symmetry do you think are in a regular octagon? (An octagon has 8 sides.) _____

Math Boxes

1. Complete.

  a. 1 yard = _____ feet

  b. $\frac{1}{3}$ yard = _____ inches

  c. 36 inches = _____ feet

  d. 72 inches = _____ yards

  e. 108 inches = _____ feet

2. Find a number in the *World Tour Book* that has 2 in the millions place. Write the number below.

_____

Round this number to the nearest hundred thousand.

_____

Read the number to a friend.

3. Draw the following angles. Use a protractor.

  a. $\angle DOB = 85°$ **b.** $\angle JMP = 170°$

4. Make a true number sentence by filling in the missing numbers.

  a. _____ = 7 + (8 * 9)

  b. 48 / 6 = 40 / _____

  c. (20 + 8) / 4 = _____

  d. (6 * 6) / 3 = _____

5. The time is 7:58 A.M. on Tuesday. What time and day of the week will it be in 47 hours and 12 minutes?

  a. Day of the week:

  _____

  b. Time:

  _____:_____ A.M. or P.M.

Use with Lesson 81.

Frieze Patterns

A **frieze pattern** is a design made of shapes lined up in a strip. Frieze patterns are often found on the outside or inside walls of buildings, on the borders of rugs and tiled floors, and on clothing.

In many frieze patterns, the same design is reflected over and over. For example, the following frieze pattern was used to decorate a sash worn by a Mazahua woman from San Felipe Santiago, in the state of New Mexico. The strange-looking beasts in the frieze are probably meant to be horses.

Some frieze patterns are made by repeating the same design, but without reflecting it. The frieze pattern looks as if it were made by sliding the design along the strip. An example of such a frieze pattern is the elephant and horse design that was found on a woman's sarong from Sumba, Indonesia. All elephants and horses are facing in the same direction.

The following frieze pattern is similar to one painted on the decorated front page of a Koran made in Egypt about 600 years ago. The Koran is the holy book of the religion of Islam. Notice that this design has not been reflected. Nor can you make the frieze by sliding the design. Rather, the design has been rotated; it looks as if it has been turned upside down.

During the next few days, look for frieze patterns on buildings, rugs, floors, and clothing. If possible, bring pictures to school, or make a sketch of friezes you find.

Use with Lesson 82.

Frieze Patterns (continued)

1. Extend the following frieze patterns. Use a straightedge or your transparent mirror to help you.

a.

b.

c.

2. Now create your own frieze pattern. Make a design in part of the box. Then repeat the design, using reflections, "slides," or rotations. When you have finished, you may wish to color or shade your frieze pattern.

Date _____ Time _____

Positive and Negative Numbers

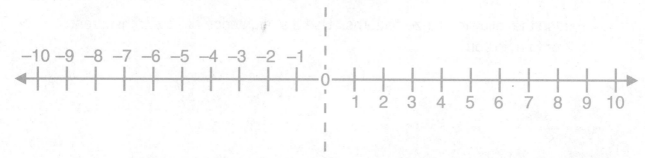

Place your transparent mirror on the line that passes through 0 on the number line above. Look through the mirror. What do you see?

The image of what negative number do you see—

above +1? _____   above +2? _____   above +8? _____

The **opposite** of every positive number is a negative number, and the opposite of every negative number is a positive number. The diagram below is another way to show that this is true.

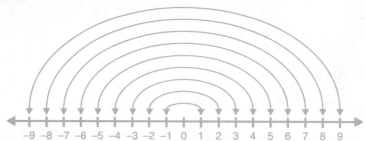

You have probably used positive and negative numbers before. For example, you use them to name temperatures: another name for 20 degrees above zero is +20°, for 5 degrees below zero, –5°.

You have also seen positive and negative numbers on a number line.

- Positive numbers are shown to the right of zero on the number line. The farther such a number is from zero, the larger the number. For example, +10 is greater than +5 because it is farther from zero.

- Negative numbers are shown to the left of zero. The farther such a number is from zero, the smaller the number. For example, –10 is less than –5 because it is farther away from zero.

Use with Lesson 83.

The Credits/Debits Game

Materials: 1 deck of regular playing cards or *Everything Math Deck* recording page (page 184)

If you are using an *Everything Math Deck*, remove the blue 11–20 cards, or keep them but mark the odd numbers with a "+" to show they are credits.

If you are using a regular deck of playing cards, remove the face cards, or keep them but mark them as 11, 12, and 13.

Number of players: 2

Directions:

1. Shuffle the deck and lay it face down between you and your partner.

2. The black numbered cards are the "credits" and the blue or red numbered cards are the "debits."

3. Each player begins at +$10.

4. You and your partner will take turns drawing a card and recording the result on journal page 184.

5. At the end of 10 draws each or at the end of the playing time, whichever comes first, the partner in the best financial position is the winner of the round.

 # Hot or Cold?

The most bizarre temperature changes in history occurred at Spearfish, South Dakota, on January 22, 1943. At 7:30 A.M. the thermometer read –4°F. By 7:32 A.M. the temperature had risen 49 degrees. By 9:00 A.M. it had drifted up to 54°F. Then, suddenly, it plunged 58 degrees in 27 minutes. What was the temperature at 9:27 A.M.?

Use with Lesson 83.

Credits/Debits Recording Sheet

-22 -21 -20 -19 -18 -17 -16 -15 -14 -13 -12 -11 -10 -9 -8 -7 -6 -5 -4 -3 -2 -1 0 +1 +2 +3 +4 +5 +6 +7 +8 +9 +10 +11 +12 +13 +14 +15 +16 +17 +18 +19 +20 +21 +22

Game 1

	Start	Change	End, and next start		
1	+$10				
2					
3					
4					
5					
6					
7					
8					
9					
10					

Game 2

	Start	Change	End, and next start		
1	+$10				
2					
3					
4					
5					
6					
7					
8					
9					
10					

Use with Lesson 83.

Math Boxes

1. Tell whether the number sentence is true or false.

   a. 52 = 10 + (6 * 7) _____

   b. 80 = (4 * 8) + (6 * 8) _____

   c. 68 > (5 * 8) + 13 _____

   d. 7 = (7 * 7) / (7 * 7) _____

2. Write a missing equivalent fraction or decimal for the values given.

Decimal		Fraction
a. 0.25	=	_____
b. _____	=	$\frac{1}{5}$
c. _____	=	$\frac{6}{12}$
d. 0.60	=	_____

3. During a recent survey, Star Elementary found out that each student eats an average of about 17 pieces of candy or junk food per week. About how many pieces of candy or junk food would this be for a classroom of 32 students?

   _____

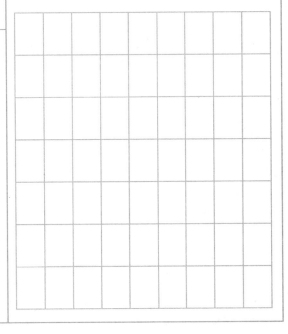

4. Round the following numbers to the nearest hundredth.

   a. 12.368 _____

   b. 234.989 _____

   c. 1.225 _____

   d. 12.304 _____

   e. 0.550 _____

Patchwork Quilts

Women in colonial times worked together to make **patchwork quilts**. Because fabric was expensive and scarce, quilts were often made out of whatever scraps of material were available. The quilters would begin by creating a square pattern out of pieces of material of various shapes, colors, and textures. Then they would make many more square patches having exactly the same pattern. When they had enough patches for a quilt, they would sew them together to form a quilt top. The women would then place the bottom piece of the quilt on a wooden frame and add a layer of lining, or batting, made out of cotton or wool. Finally, they would spread the quilt top over the batting and, with tiny stitches, sew the quilt top to the batting and the bottom piece.

The quilt was put together at a party, called a **quilting bee**. While cutting and sewing, the women would tell stories and share what went on in their lives. When the quilt was finished, the women were joined by the men for supper and dancing.

Many patchwork patterns have become traditions. Their names and designs came from the everyday lives of the people who created them. For example, the "Buggy Wheel" pattern was probably inspired by a trip in a buggy. Along with walking or riding a horse, this was a popular form of transportation in early America.

Buggy Wheel

Although early quilters may not have known much about geometry, we can see it at work in many of their designs. Patchwork quilting involves the cutting of fabric into various geometric shapes and sewing them together into patterns. The pattern may be repeated over and over in forming a quilt; or it may be rotated or reflected as the patches are assembled. Many patchwork patterns, such as the "Buggy Wheel" and "Does and Darts" patterns, are symmetric. Others, like the "Crazy Quilt," seem to have been created at random.

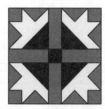

Does and Darts

Crazy Quilt

The beauty of a quilt lies in its uniqueness. No two patches need ever be the same, because there are so many possible arrangements of fabrics and colors.

Use with Lesson 84.

Symmetric Patterns

Each pattern to the right of the Pinwheel pattern has been colored in three different ways. Notice how each color arrangement changes the number of lines of symmetry.

Pinwheel Pattern

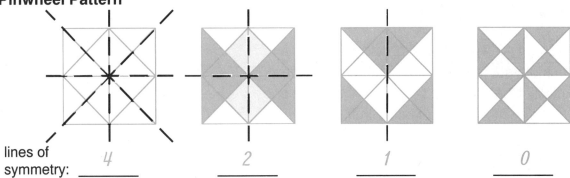

lines of
symmetry: ___4___   ___2___   ___1___   ___0___

For each pattern below, draw all the lines of symmetry and record the number of lines of symmetry.

---

1. Bow-Tie Pattern

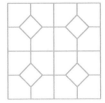 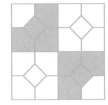 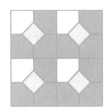 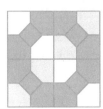

lines of
symmetry: _____   _____   _____   _____

---

2. Ohio Star Pattern

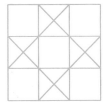 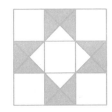 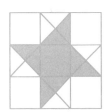 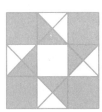

lines of
symmetry: _____   _____   _____   _____

---

3. Pineapple Log Cabin Pattern

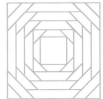   

lines of
symmetry: _____   _____   _____   _____

Use with Lesson 84.

Traditional 9-Patch Patterns

Some patterns, called **9-patch patterns**, look like they are made up of 9 squares. You can make your own 9-patch pattern by arranging square, triangle, and rectangle pieces on a 3-by-3 grid.

Tear out Activity Sheets 18 and 19 from the back of your journal. Cut out the squares on Activity Sheet 18 and color half of them in one color and the other half in another color. Then make triangles by cutting each of 6 of the squares in half along a diagonal. Make rectangles by cutting 6 other squares in half.

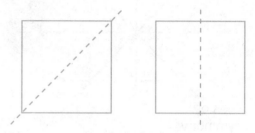

Now arrange some of the pieces on the grid on Activity Sheet 19. When you have completed a pattern, draw it and color it on one of the 3-by-3 squares below.

1. Make 1 or 2 patterns having 4 lines of symmetry.

 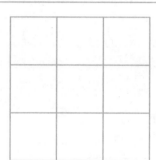

2. Make 1 or 2 patterns having 2 lines of symmetry.

 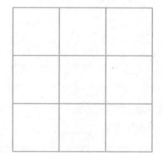

3. Make 1 or 2 patterns having no lines of symmetry.

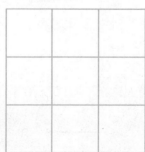 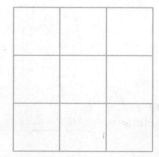

Use with Lesson 84.

Rotating Patterns

Many traditional American quilts are made by rotating the square patterns, as they are assembled into a quilt.

The first patchwork pattern below is a variation of the traditional "Grandmother's Fan" pattern. The patterns to the right of it show the pattern after it has been rotated clockwise a $\frac{1}{4}$-, $\frac{1}{2}$-, and $\frac{3}{4}$-turn.

   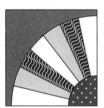

This is what part of the quilt might look like if some of the patterns had been rotated.

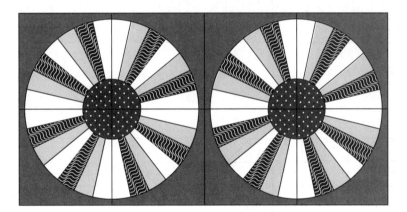

The "Wrench" pattern at the right, also known as the "Monkey Wrench," is a classic pattern which can be found in Amish and Mennonite quilts. Describe what it would look like after it has been rotated a $\frac{1}{4}$-, $\frac{1}{2}$-, and $\frac{3}{4}$-turn.

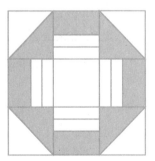

_____

_____

How many lines of symmetry does it have? _____

Making a Quilt

As you study the traditional 9-patch patterns on this page, think about the following questions:

- Do you see where some of the patterns might have gotten their names?

- What are some similarities and differences among the patterns?

- How many lines of symmetry does each pattern have?

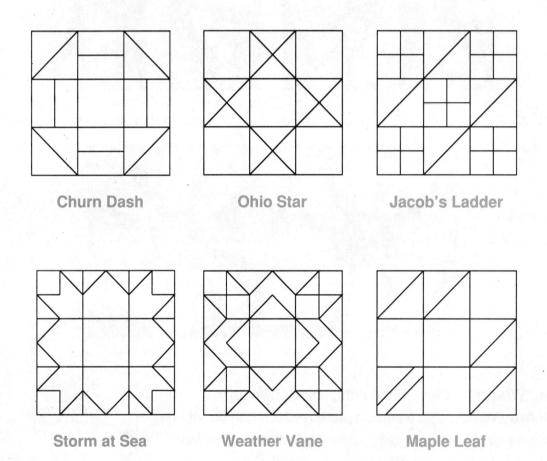

Churn Dash   Ohio Star   Jacob's Ladder

Storm at Sea   Weather Vane   Maple Leaf

Making a Quilt (continued)

Work with two of your classmates to make a quilt.

Tear out Activity Sheets 22–25 from the back of your journal. Cut out the 3-by-3 square on each of Activity Sheets 22–24. Punch holes through the dots along the borders. Cut out the pieces on Activity Sheet 25.

You and your partners choose one of the patterns. Decide on a way to color it. The colored pattern the group chooses **should not have more than 2 lines of symmetry**. Then each of you copy this design on each of your 3-by-3 squares. You can use the pieces you cut out to trace the pattern on the 3-by-3 squares. Or you may trace the shapes onto colored paper, cut them out, and paste them on the 3-by-3 squares. Your group should end up with nine 3-by-3 square patches that look exactly alike.

Lay all nine square patches on the floor and arrange them so that some of the square patterns have been be rotated. When your group has agreed on an arrangement, line up the holes on the edges of the squares. Then fasten the pieces together by weaving yarn in and out of the holes. If you choose to, you may make a ruffle for your quilt out of a strip of crepe paper. Pleat and glue it around the edges of the border.

Here is an example of a quilt made out of the Maple Leaf pattern.

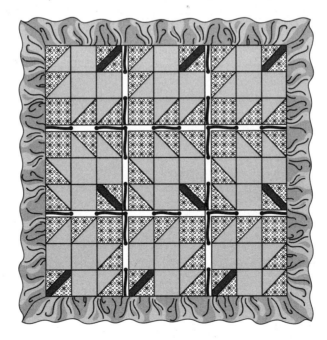

Use with Lesson 84.

Date _____ Time _____

Title: _____

REGION 5

Canada

United States

Mexico   Cuba   Haiti

Jamaica

Guatemala
El Salvador
Costa Rica
Panama

Color Code

	blue
	green
	red
	yellow

Russia

Turkey

Iran

China

Japan

India

Bangladesh

Vietnam

Thailand

REGION 4

Venezuela

Colombia

Ecuador

Brazil

Peru

Bolivia

Paraguay

Chile

Argentina

Uruguay

Australia

REGION 3

Literacy and Standard of Living

1. List all the countries that are colored blue on the Standard-of-Living map.

   _____

   _____

2. List all the countries that are colored blue on the Literacy map.

   _____

   _____

3. Which region seems to have the highest standard of living?   _____

4. Which region seems to have the most literate population?   _____

5. Which region seems to have the lowest standard of living?   _____

6. Which region seems to have the least literate population?   _____

7. How many countries are the same color on both maps?   _____

8. How many countries are blue on one map and green on the other?   _____

   How many are green on one map and red on the other?   _____

   How many are red on one map and yellow on the other?   _____

9. Do you think countries with large areas have an advantage over small
   countries? Explain your answer.

   _____

   _____

   _____

   _____

Use with Lesson 85.

Date _____ Time _____

Math Boxes

1. Peter had 12 dimes. He spent $\frac{2}{3}$ of his money on a soda and the rest on candy.

    a. How much did the soda cost? _____

    b. How much did the candy cost? _____

    c. What fraction of the total did the candy cost? _____

    d. How much would Peter spend if he spent $\frac{5}{6}$ of his money? _____

2. Solve.

    a.   7 8 9
         $-$ 4 9 2

    b.   2 3 9 0
          $+$ 6 8 9

3. Round the following numbers to the nearest hundred.

    a. 8932 _____

    b. 45,056 _____

    c. 1,306,952 _____

    d. 400,579 _____

4. In the Northwest Regional Conference, the top 10 players had the following high scores in a basketball game:

    25   17   42   28   26   21   26   38   18   15

    Find the following landmarks:

    Median: _____   Minimum: _____   Range: _____

    Mode: _____   Maximum: _____

Use with Lesson 85.

Nutrition Facts
Serving Size 1 Cookie (26g/0.9 oz.)
Servings Per Container 10

Amount Per Serving

Calories 130   Calories from Fat 50

	% Daily Value*
Total Fat 6g	
Saturated Fat 2.5g	9%
Polyunsaturated Fat 0g	13%
Monounsaturated Fat 2.5g	
Cholesterol 10mg	
Sodium 35mg	3%
Total Carbohydrate 16g	1%
Dietary Fiber 2g	5%
Sugars 9g	8%
Protein 1g	

Amtrak Set to Cut Service 21%

Sale—50% Off Everything Must Go

For Wednesday, there is a 30% chance of showers.

You can get a furnace filter that captures 94 percent of the dust, dander, pollen, and other particles that float through your house.

Voter Turnout Pegged at 55% of Registered Voters

Raisin-Lite Cookies
50% Less Fat
than our regular cookies

At present, computers are a leading cause of increased demand for electrical power, accounting for an estimated 5 percent of commercial demand.

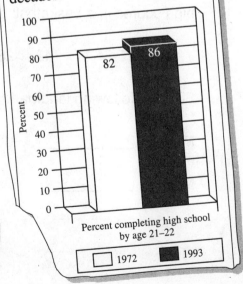

Staying in School

Newly released Education Department figures show that high school completion rates have grown over the last two decades.

Percent completing high school by age 21–22

☐ 1972   ■ 1993

Total attendance was 8% higher than in the previous year.

Many Names for Percents

Choose five of the percent examples on page 196. Copy each statement.   Fill in the "100% box." Show the percent by shading the 10-by-10 square. Then write other names for the percent by filling in the missing information next to the 10-by-10 square.

Example: Last season, Duncan made 62 percent of his shots.

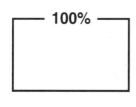

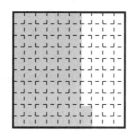

That's ____*62*____ out of every 100.

Fraction name: $\dfrac{\boxed{62}}{100}$

Decimal name: ___*0.62*___

---

1. **Statement:** _____

_____

_____

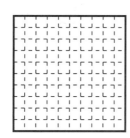

That's _____ out of every 100.

Fraction name: $\dfrac{\Box}{100}$

Decimal name: _____

---

2. **Statement:** _____

_____

_____

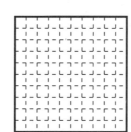

That's _____ out of every 100.

Fraction name: $\dfrac{\Box}{100}$

Decimal name: _____

Use with Lesson 86.

Many Names for Percents (continued)

3. Statement: _____

_____

_____

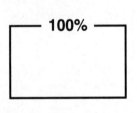   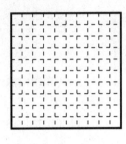

That's _____ out of every 100.

Fraction name: $\frac{\boxed{}}{100}$

Decimal name: _____

---

4. Statement: _____

_____

_____

100%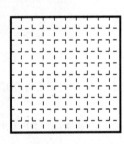

That's _____ out of every 100.

Fraction name: $\frac{\boxed{}}{100}$

Decimal name: _____

---

5. Statement: _____

_____

_____

100%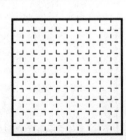

That's _____ out of every 100.

Fraction name: $\frac{\boxed{}}{100}$

Decimal name: _____

Use with Lesson 86.

Math Boxes

1. Solve.

  a. 256 * 9 = _____

  b. 91 * 37 = _____

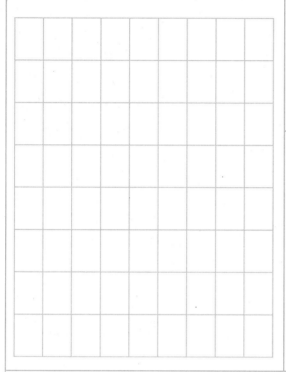

2. It takes Peter about 30 minutes to get ready for school. The bus picks him up at about 7:38 A.M. If he wakes up at 7:04, will he have enough time to get ready?

_____

At what time will he be ready?

_____:_____

3. Round 36,590,421 to the—

  nearest ten   _____

  nearest thousand _____

  nearest million   _____

4. Find the solution of each open sentence. Write a number sentence with the solution in place of the variable.

Open Sentence	Solution	Number Sentence
a. 42 + x = 68	x = _____	_____
b. a = 199 − 5	a = _____	_____
c. 54 = 6 * s	s = _____	_____
d. 45 + y = 105	y = _____	_____

Date _____ Time _____

Math Message

Alfred, Nadine, Kyla, and Jackson each took the same math test. There were 20 problems on the test.

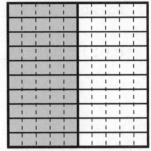
100%
20-problem test

1. Alfred missed $\frac{1}{2}$ of the problems.
   He missed **0.50** of the problems.
   That's **50%** of the problems.

   How many problems did he miss? _____

   $\frac{1}{2}$ of 20 = _____

   50% of 20 = _____

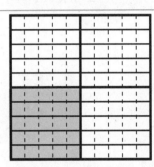

$\frac{1}{2}$ or 50% is shaded.

2. Nadine missed $\frac{1}{4}$ of the problems.
   She missed **0.25** of the problems.
   That's **25%** of the problems.

   How many problems did she miss? _____

   $\frac{1}{4}$ of 20 = _____

   25% of 20 = _____

$\frac{1}{4}$ or 25% is shaded.

3. Kyla missed $\frac{1}{10}$ of the problems.
   She missed **0.10** of the problems.
   That's **10%** of the problems.

   How many problems did she miss? _____

   $\frac{1}{10}$ of 20 = _____

   10% of 20 = _____

$\frac{1}{10}$ or 10% is shaded.

4. Jackson missed $\frac{1}{5}$ of the problems.
   He missed **0.20** of the problems.
   That's **20%** of the problems.

   How many problems did he miss? _____

   $\frac{1}{5}$ of 20 = _____

   20% of 20 = _____

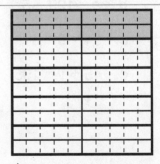

$\frac{1}{5}$ or 20% is shaded.

Use with Lesson 87.

Date _____ Time _____

Fractions, Decimals, and Percents

Fill in the missing numbers.
Problem 1 is done for you.

```
┌── 100% ──┐
│          │
│  large square  │
│          │
└──────────┘
```

1. Ways of showing $\frac{3}{4}$:

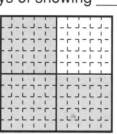

$\dfrac{3}{4}$ is shaded. $\dfrac{75}{100}$

0.<u>75</u>   <u>75</u> %

2. Ways of showing _____ :

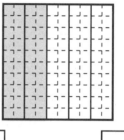

$\dfrac{\boxed{}}{5}$ is shaded. $\dfrac{\boxed{}}{100}$

0._____   _____%

3. Ways of showing _____ :

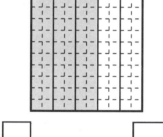

$\dfrac{\boxed{}}{5}$ is shaded. $\dfrac{\boxed{}}{100}$

0._____   _____%

4. Ways of showing _____ :

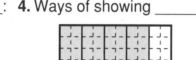

$\dfrac{\boxed{}}{5}$ is shaded. $\dfrac{\boxed{}}{100}$

0._____   _____%

5. Ways of showing _____ :

$\dfrac{\boxed{}}{5}$ is shaded. $\dfrac{\boxed{}}{100}$

_____   _____%

6. Ways of showing _____ :

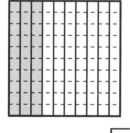

$\dfrac{3}{\boxed{}}$ is shaded. $\dfrac{\boxed{}}{100}$

0._____   _____%

7. Ways of showing _____ :

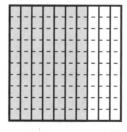

$\dfrac{7}{\boxed{}}$ is shaded. $\dfrac{\boxed{}}{100}$

0._____   _____%

8. Ways of showing _____ :

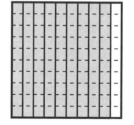

$\dfrac{9}{\boxed{}}$ is shaded. $\dfrac{\boxed{}}{100}$

0._____   _____%

Use with Lesson 87.

Date _____ Time _____

Calculator Decimals

1. Use your calculator to rename each fraction as a decimal.

$\frac{1}{2}$ =	0	.	5					$\frac{1}{14}$ =			
$\frac{1}{3}$ =	0	.	3	3	3	3	3	3	$\frac{1}{15}$ =		
$\frac{1}{4}$ =									$\frac{1}{16}$ =		
$\frac{1}{5}$ =									$\frac{1}{17}$ =		
$\frac{1}{6}$ =									$\frac{1}{18}$ =		
$\frac{1}{7}$ =									$\frac{1}{19}$ =		
$\frac{1}{8}$ =									$\frac{1}{20}$ =		
$\frac{1}{9}$ =									$\frac{1}{21}$ =		
$\frac{1}{10}$ =									$\frac{1}{22}$ =		
$\frac{1}{11}$ =									$\frac{1}{23}$ =		
$\frac{1}{12}$ =									$\frac{1}{24}$ =		
$\frac{1}{13}$ =									$\frac{1}{25}$ =		

2. Make up some of your own.

$\frac{1}{}$ =			$\frac{1}{}$ =		
$\frac{1}{}$ =			$\frac{1}{}$ =		
$\frac{1}{}$ =			$\frac{1}{}$ =		
$\frac{1}{}$ =			$\frac{1}{}$ =		
$\frac{1}{}$ =			$\frac{1}{}$ =		

Use with Lesson 88.

Fraction/Percent Concentration

Materials: 1 set of Fraction/Percent tiles (Activity Sheet 24)

Number of players: 2 or 3

Directions:

Place the tiles facedown on the playing surface and mix them up.

Players take turns. At each turn, a player turns over a fraction and a percent tile. If the fraction and percent are equivalent, the player keeps the tiles. If the tiles do not match, the player turns the tiles facedown.

Players use a calculator to check each other's matches. A player who makes a mistake loses his or her next turn.

The game ends when all tiles have been taken. The player with the most tiles wins.

 Terrific Pacific

The area of the largest ocean in the world, the Pacific, is about 64.2 million square miles. That's about 45.9% of the area of all the oceans in the world.

Source: Matthews, Peter, ed. *The Guinness Book of Records 1993*. New York: Guinness Publishing Ltd., 1992.

Use with Lesson 88.

Date _____ Time _____

Math Boxes

1. If you use about 7 sheets of paper per day, about how many would you use in:

1 week? _____

4 weeks? _____

52 weeks? _____

2. Find the flag of Hungary on page 32 of your *World Tour Book*. Be sure to consider color as you answer the following questions.

  a. Does this flag have a vertical line of symmetry? _____

  b. Does it have a horizontal line of symmetry? _____

3. Fill in the missing numbers on the number lines.

  a.

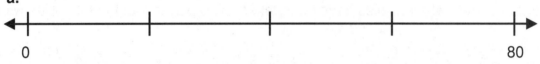

0   80

_____   _____   _____

  b.

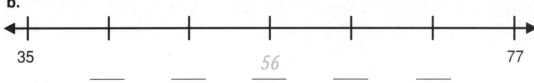

35   *56*   77

_____   _____   _____   _____   _____

4. Measure the line segment to the nearest $\frac{1}{4}$ inch.

_____

_____ inches

Draw a line segment that is about half the length of the one above. Record its length.

length = about _____ inches

Date _____ Time _____

Discount Number Stories

1. A store is offering a **discount** of 10% on all items. This means that you save $\frac{1}{10}$ of the **regular price**. Find the sale price of each item. (The **sale price** is the amount you pay after subtracting the discount from the regular price.)

Item	Regular price	Discount	Sale price
CD player	$140	$14	
giant screen TV	$1200		
radio	$75		
cassette player		$3	

2. An airline offers a 25% discount on the regular airfare for tickets purchased at least 1 month in advance. Find the discounted price of each ticket.

Regular airfare	Discount	Discounted price
$400	$100	
$240		
	$75	

3. An encyclopedia can be purchased at a 30% discount if it is ordered before April 1. On April 1, the regular price of $400 will be charged.

   If you order it before April 1:

   a. How much will you save? _____

   b. How much will you pay? _____

Challenge

4. A refrigerator can be paid for in 12 monthly installments of $50 each. If you pay for it all at once, you save 25% of what you would pay if you buy it on the installment plan.

   How much will the refrigerator cost if you pay for it all at once? _____

Use with Lesson 89.

Math Boxes

1. During the school play at Gilbert Elementary, the auditorium was filled with 850 students. 489 of the students were girls. How many were boys?

_____

2. Make a true number sentence by inserting parentheses.

   a. 8 * 2 + 20 = 36

   b. 63 = 9 / 3 * 21

   c. 28 / 7 * 4 = 16

   d. 10 / 5 * 2 = 1

3. Shade more than $\frac{3}{4}$ but less than the whole square. Write the fraction and decimal for the amount shaded.

Fraction: _____

Decimal: _____

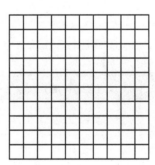

4. Write 5 other names for 0.25.

   a. _____

   b. _____

   c. _____

   d. _____

   e. _____

6. Subtract.

   a.   9 8 3
       − 4 9 4

   b.   7 0 0
       − 2 9 9

Date _____ Time _____

Math Boxes

1. Twenty-nine students in Ms. Wright's class each brought 50 bottle caps they had collected. How many bottle caps in all did the class bring?

   _____

2. Complete.

   3 ft = _____ in

   6 ft 3 in = _____ in

   2 yr. = _____ mo.

   7 yr. 6 mo. = _____ mo.

   3 lb = _____ oz

3. Find two flags on page 32 of your *World Tour Book* that have both horizontal and vertical symmetry. (Remember that the colors must also be symmetric.)

   a. _____

   b. _____

4. Fill in the missing numbers on the number lines.

   a.

   0   1

   b.

   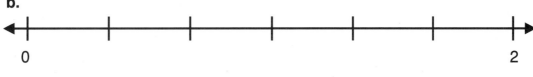

   0   2

Date _____ Time _____

Trivia Survey Results

1. Tabulate the results of the trivia survey for the whole class. Wait for directions from your teacher.

Question	Yes	No	Total	Yes/Total	Percent "Yes"
1. Is Monday your favorite day?					
2. Have you gone out to the movies in the last month?					
3. Did you eat breakfast today?					
4. Do you keep a map in your car?					
5. Did you eat at a fast-food restaurant yesterday?					
6. Did you read a book during the last month?					
7. Are you more than 1 meter tall?					
8. Do you like liver?					

2. On the basis of the survey results, is it more likely that a person will—

   Read a book or go to a movie? _____

   Eat breakfast or eat in a fast-food restaurant? _____

   Like liver or like Mondays? _____

Date _____ Time _____

Math Boxes

Create a graph that represents data with the following landmarks. Use at least 10 numbers.

Mode: 39   Median: 35   Minimum: 7   Range: 36

Use with Lesson 91.

The Amazon Rainforest

Read the article about the Amazon rainforest on pages 10 and 11 of the *World Tour Book.*

1. Why is the Amazon rainforest being cleared? List as many reasons as you can.

   _____

   _____

   _____

   _____

   _____

   _____

2. What are some of the consequences of the loss of the rainforest?

   _____

   _____

   _____

   _____

   _____

   _____

Excessive Diet

In one day Americans eat 815 billion calories of food—roughly 200 billion more than they need to maintain a moderate level of activity. That's enough extra calories to feed everyone in Mexico, a country of 80 million people.

Use with Lesson 92.

The Amazon Rainforest (continued)

The Amazon rainforest is not the only tropical forest that is being destroyed. **Deforestation**, the clearing of forest land, is also taking place in other parts of the world. Each circle below represents all of the forest land that was left in that country in 1990. The shaded part shows the percent of forest land expected to be cleared between 1990 and the year 2000.

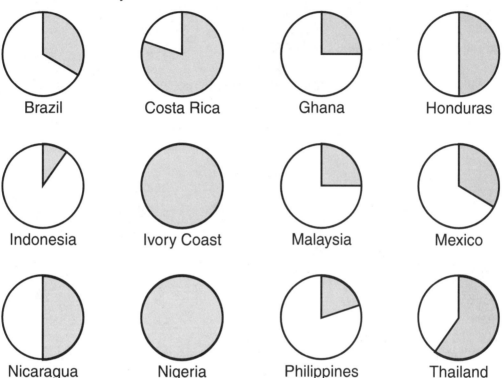

Brazil	Costa Rica	Ghana	Honduras
Indonesia	Ivory Coast	Malaysia	Mexico
Nicaragua	Nigeria	Philippines	Thailand

Which countries are expected to lose about:

1. 100% of their forests?   _____

2. 50% of their forests?   _____

3. 25% of their forests?   _____

4. Less than 25% of their forests? _____

5. Between 25% and 50% of their forests? _____

6. Between 50% and 75% of their forests? _____

7. Between 75% and 100% of their forests? _____

Use with Lesson 92.

Math Message

1. **a.** Circle $\frac{1}{10}$ of the dimes.

b. What amount of money did you circle? Write this as a decimal. $_____

c. How many pennies are there in $\frac{1}{10}$ of a dollar? _____

2. **a.** Circle $\frac{1}{2}$ of the dimes.

b. What amount of money did you circle? Write this as a decimal. $_____

c. How many pennies are there in $\frac{1}{2}$ of a dollar? _____

3. **a.** Circle $\frac{3}{5}$ of the dimes.

b. What amount of money did you circle? Write this as a decimal. $_____

c. How many pennies are there in $\frac{3}{5}$ of a dollar? _____

Amazing Mammals

There are many different kinds of mammals. Elephants, mice, horses, kangaroos, dolphins, humans—all are mammals. The smallest mammal, the pygmy shrew, weighs about as much as a dime. The largest mammal, the blue whale, may be the largest creature that ever lived.

Mammals are found almost everywhere on Earth. Arctic hares, polar bears, and seals thrive in the intense cold of the far north. Camels, foxes, and gerbils live in scorching desert heat. Whales roam the oceans far from land.

One reason that mammals survive in so many different environments is that they can keep their body temperatures high and almost constant. They are warm-blooded, unlike reptiles (such as snakes), amphibians (such as frogs), and fish. Cold-blooded animals take on the temperature of their surroundings.

Many mammals, such as bears, dogs, and cats, stay warm with the help of a covering of hair (usually called fur). Mammals are the only animals with hair.

Some mammals, such as whales and humans, depend on a layer of fat to keep from losing heat. Mammals also shiver or move around to help keep warm.

Some mammals—especially humans—cool off in hot weather by sweating. African elephants flap their huge ears. Dogs pant, using their lungs to help remove heat from their bodies.

Most mammals are carried inside the female until they are born. Reptiles, amphibians, fish, and birds all develop from eggs outside the animal. A few mammals, such as platypuses, also hatch from eggs.

The biggest difference from other animals is that female mammals can feed their babies with milk from their own bodies. No other animals do this.

Most mammals have abilities suited to their habitat. Prairie dogs, gophers, and rabbits are skilled at burrowing. Tigers see very well at night. One type of mammal has even learned how to fly. (Can you name it?) Many mammals, including whales and elephants, have sophisticated communication abilities.

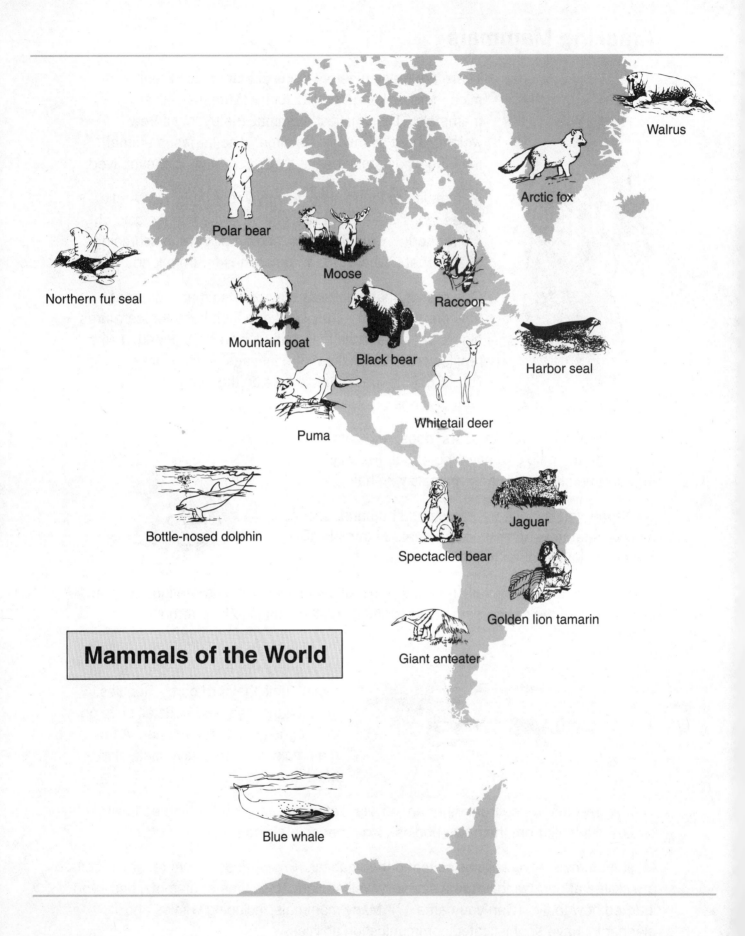

Walrus

Arctic fox

Polar bear

Moose

Raccoon

Northern fur seal

Mountain goat

Black bear

Harbor seal

Puma

Whitetail deer

Bottle-nosed dolphin

Spectacled bear

Jaguar

Golden lion tamarin

Mammals of the World

Giant anteater

Blue whale

Red squirrel

Hedgehog

Gray wolf

Wildcat

Roe deer

North African gerbil

One-hump camel

Snow leopard

Two-hump camel

Siberian tiger

Giant panda

African elephant

Lion

Asian elephant

Orangutan

Mountain gorilla

Hippopotamus

Platypus

Red kangaroo

Zebra

Giraffe

Koala

Orca (killer whale)

Leopard seal

Amazing Mammals (continued)

All mammals have **vertebrae** (backbones). All mammals breathe air (unlike fish, which take oxygen out of water that passes through their gills). Some mammals can stay underwater for a long time, but eventually they must come up for air. (Which mammals are they?)

Mammals have large, well-developed brains. They can learn from their experiences. Some, such as horses and elephants, can be trained to do work. Others can be trained to entertain (as in a circus) or to be companions (especially dogs and cats). Some scientists believe that the challenge of living in harsh environments has made mammals quite intelligent.

Of all the different **species** (kinds) of mammals, almost one half are rodents (such as rats and mice). Almost one fourth are various types of bats.

You are a mammal. How do you compare with other mammals?

 ## Amazing Mammal Facts

- In one night, a mole can dig a 300-foot tunnel.
- Camels aren't the only mammals that can go a long time without water. In fact, both a giraffe and a rat can go without water longer than a camel can. Kangaroo rats never drink water; they produce fluids from the food they eat and the air they breathe.
- Sixty cows can produce a ton of milk in less than one day.

Source: Louis, David. *2201 Fascinating Facts.* New York: Greenwich House, 1983.

Use with Lesson 94.

Mammal Measures

Find three interesting measurement facts about mammals (other than humans). Look in encyclopedias, almanacs, books, magazines, or other sources. For example, you could look up the size and weight of your favorite mammals, or find out how much they eat, how long they sleep, or how far they travel in a day.

Record the measurement facts in the spaces on the next three pages. Include the names of your sources and the pages where you found the facts. Then think about each fact and give your opinion on the following questions:

1. How do you think the measuring was done?

2. Is the measure for **just one specific animal**?

   Example: The oldest known gorilla lived for 39 years 4 months.

   Or, is the fact a **range** of measures? The measure for any one animal would be between the smallest and largest measures in the range.

   Example: An adult gray wolf weighs 70 to 120 pounds.

   Or, is the measure a "typical" or "average" value for many animals?

   Example: The top speed of a grizzly bear is 30 miles per hour.

   Might it be a **guess**, because the actual measuring would be hard or impossible to do?

3. Compare yourself with the mammal, using this measure.

   Example: "I weigh twice as much."

Amazing Mammal Measures

- A giraffe's tongue is about 18 inches long.
- A full-grown moose may be 8 feet high at the shoulder and have antlers that stretch 7 feet across.
- A hippopotamus may open its mouth wide enough for a child 4 feet tall to stand inside.

Source: Louis, David. *2201 Fascinating Facts.* New York: Greenwich House, 1983.

Use with Lesson 94.

Date _____ Time _____

Mammal Measures: Fact 1

Mammal(s): _____

Source: _____

Measurement fact: _____

_____

_____

_____

How might this measurement be done?

_____

_____

How would you describe Measurement Fact 1? Check one, or write your own description.

_____ the measure of a single animal

_____ a range of measures

_____ a typical or average measure

_____ a guess

_____ _____

Compare yourself with the mammal, using Measurement Fact 1.

_____

_____

_____

Mammal Measures: Fact 2

Mammal(s): _____

Source: _____

Measurement fact: _____

_____

_____

_____

How might this measurement be done?

_____

_____

How would you describe Measurement Fact 2? Check one, or write your own description.

_____ the measure of a single animal

_____ a range of measures

_____ a typical or average measure

_____ a guess

_____ _____

Compare yourself with the mammal, using Measurement Fact 2.

_____

_____

_____

Use with Lesson 94.

Date _____ Time _____

Mammal Measures: Fact 3

Mammal(s): _____

Source: _____

Measurement fact: _____

_____

_____

_____

How might this measurement be done?

_____

_____

How would you describe Measurement Fact 3? Check one, or write your own
description.

_____ the measure of a single animal

_____ a range of measures

_____ a typical or average measure

_____ a guess

_____ _____

Compare yourself with the mammal, using Measurement Fact 3.

_____

_____

_____

Math Boxes

1. Bill, Martha, Monique, and Louis each participate in different after-school activities three times per week: hockey, dance, gymnastics, or swimming.
   - Louis wears a lot of equipment for protection during his after-school activity.
   - Martha wears tights and leotards for her after-school activity.
   - Bill does not like to dance or be in the water.

   Which after-school activity does each like the best?

   Bill _____   Louis _____

   Monique _____   Martha _____

2. Complete.

   3 ft = _____ in

   2 ft 7 in = _____ in

   5 yd = _____ ft

   4 yd 2 ft = _____ ft

3. Give 3 equivalent fractions for each of the following.

   a. $\frac{1}{2}$ = _____ _____ _____

   b. $\frac{3}{5}$ = _____ _____ _____

   c. $\frac{3}{3}$ = _____ _____ _____

   d. $\frac{7}{8}$ = _____ _____ _____

4. A store is giving a 20% discount on all items. Find the discounted price for each.

Item	Regular price	Discounted price
CD	$15.00	_____
Microwave oven	$110.00	_____
Computer	$2000.00	_____
Printer	$375.00	_____

Use with Lesson 94.

Mammal Speeds

Introduction

The speed at which mammals walk or run is important for many of them. It helps them avoid or run from danger. Speed also helps predators when they hunt other animals for food. It helps mammals when they search for food, water, or shelter.

The speed of mammals varies widely. The fastest mammals, including some antelopes and gazelles, can run two to three times as fast as the fastest human. On the other hand, some mammals move very slowly. Can you think of any? (A turtle is not a mammal.) A three-toed sloth might take 20 minutes to travel the length of a football field (if it kept moving).

Some mammals can maintain fast speeds for long distances. Antelopes, zebras, and horses, as well as dolphins and whales, can travel for hours at average speeds of 20 miles per hour or more. Most mammals, however, are not marathon runners. They are sprinters, built to move quickly over short distances.

How does your speed compare with the speed of other mammals?

It couldn't happen, of course, but suppose that you, an elephant, and a cheetah were to race a distance of 100 yards, or 300 feet. Which of you would win? Which would come in second? third?

My Prediction: First _____   Second _____   Third _____

On the line below, show the winner crossing the finish line. (Use "C" for the cheetah, "E" for the elephant, and "Me" for yourself.) Show where you think the second-place and third-place mammals will be when the fastest mammal crosses the finish line.

0	30	60	90	120	150	180	210	240	270	300 feet

Start   Finish

What information would help you predict the winner? _____

_____

Use with Lesson 95.

Mammal Speeds (continued)

Check whether your prediction is correct.

The table below will help you figure out who would win the race and by how much.

Top Sprint Speeds (Approximate) in feet per second

Fourth grader .... 20 ft/sec   Polar bear .... 58 ft/sec

Squirrel .... 18 ft/sec   Elephant .... 36 ft/sec

House cat .... 45 ft/sec   Quarter horse ..... 70 ft/sec

Cheetah .... 102 ft/sec   Fast person .... 30 ft/sec

Source (for nonhumans): *International Wildlife*. Vienna, VA: National Wildlife Federation, September-October, 1989.

Rewrite the above data in the Mammal Speed Table below. Put the fastest mammal first, the second-fastest second, and so on.

Mammal Speed Table		
	Mammal	**Top Sprint Speed (Approximate)**
1		ft/sec
2		ft/sec
3		ft/sec
4		ft/sec
5		ft/sec
6		ft/sec
7		ft/sec
8		ft/sec

Use with Lesson 95.

Mammal Speeds (continued)

According to these figures, how would the 300-foot race between an elephant, a cheetah, and a fourth grader turn out?

First _____   Second _____   Third _____

About how long does the winner
of the race take to run 300 feet?   _____ seconds

About how far do the second-place and third-place mammals run in the time it takes the winner to run 300 feet?

Second-place mammal   _____ feet

Third-place mammal   _____ feet

Would it be a close race?   _____

Draw a diagram of your findings. On the line below, show which mammal will win the race and where you think the second-place and third-place mammals will be when the fastest mammal crosses the finish line.

```
|    |    |    |    |    |    |    |    |    |    |
0    30   60   90   120  150  180  210  240  270  300 feet
Start                                            Finish
```

How good was your prediction? _____

Black and White Delight

The zebra is one of the most beautiful mammals. It is the only mammal with black-and-white stripes. Each zebra has a different set of stripes—like fingerprints on a human. In the past, people sometimes used zebras to pull carriages because of their unusual appearance. Wild zebras live only in Africa, in small herds. They must constantly watch for lions and other predators, and be prepared to run from them. A baby zebra has very long legs. Within a few minutes after it is born, it can run as fast as the rest of the herd to flee danger.

Mammal Speeds (continued)

About how many times faster is the first-place mammal than the second-place mammal?

_____

than the third-place mammal?

_____

According to the Mammal Speed Table, a fourth grader can run faster than a squirrel. Does this mean that you could catch a squirrel by running after it? Why or why not?

_____

_____

_____

_____

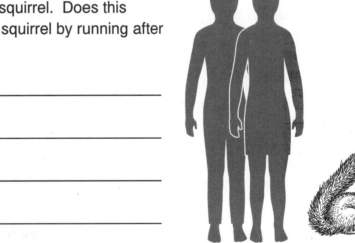

 ## Speed Demons and Slow Pokes

A frigate bird may fly as fast as 260 miles per hour. For comparison, a snail travels at a speed of about 0.0004 miles per hour.

Source: Louis, David. *2201 Fascinating Facts.* New York: Greenwich House, 1983.

Date _____ Time _____

Math Boxes

1. The class started their test at 10:10 A.M. "You have exactly $\frac{3}{4}$ of an hour," their teacher told them. At what time will they stop? _____	**2.** Write the following numbers using digits: 5 million, two hundred sixty-eight thousand, four _____ two hundred million, 3 thousand, eighty-eight _____

3. A number has
     2 hundreds
     7 tenths
     0 thousands
     1 hundred thousand
     6 hundredths
     4 ones
     5 tens
     3 ten thousands
 	
 Write the number. _____
	4. Juan collected 34 pennies each week for 52 weeks. How many pennies did Juan collect? Use a computation grid if necessary.
	
	 _____

5. Fonzi missed $\frac{1}{5}$ of the problems on his social studies test. There were 30 problems on the test. How many problems did he miss? _____ $\frac{1}{5}$ of 30 = _____ 20% of 30 = _____	**6.** Round the following numbers to the nearest hundred thousand. **a.** 37,609,034 _____ **b.** 9,540,234 _____ **c.** 290,696,332 _____ **d.** 78,291,554 _____

Use with Lesson 95.

Date _____ Time _____

Mammal Lengths and Weights

Mammal Shapes and Sizes

Mammals come in all shapes and sizes. The blue whale is between 80 and 100 feet long 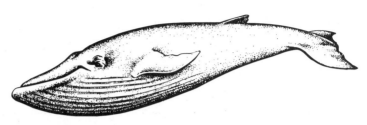 and weighs between 200,000 and 300,000 pounds. It is longer than the biggest dinosaur ever found and up to twice as heavy. The pygmy shrew, which lives in the north central United States, weighs about $\frac{1}{8}$ ounce. The hognose "bumblebee" bat from the southwest weighs about $\frac{3}{4}$ ounce. Both have bodies about 2 inches long.

 These are extremes. Most mammals can be placed in one of three size categories. For example:

Large: elephants, rhinoceroses, giraffes, hippopotamuses, horses, gorillas

Medium: deer, cows, sheep, goats, coyotes

Small: rabbits, foxes, house cats, raccoons, skunks, squirrels, hamsters, mice

Some mammals, such as bears and wild cats, are in more than one category depending on their type and size.

Compared with other mammals, are you tall or short? heavy or light? big or small?

_____

_____

_____

_____

Use with Lesson 96.

Date _____ Time _____

Mammal Lengths, Part 1

How do you compare with other mammals?

If you know your height, write it below. Otherwise, use the measure of a "typical fourth grader" from the table below.

Height: _____ inches   or   _____ centimeters

How tall are other mammals?

You stand on two legs, but most mammals go about on four legs. A mammal's height (distance from the ground to its highest point) may be considerably less than its length.

Study Link 95 listed several ways to measure the length of a mammal. Use this rule: **length of leg plus length of body and head**. Then it makes sense to compare your height with the lengths of various mammals.

Typical Lengths (length of leg plus length of body and head)					
Mammal	inches	centimeters	Mammal	inches	centimeters
Giraffe	230	580	Tiger	65	170
African elephant	210	530	Fourth grader	52	130
Asian elephant	150	380	Sheep	40	100
Arabian camel	130	330	Raccoon	20	50
Bison	110	280	Rabbit	12	30
Zebra	100	250	House Cat	10	25
Mountain gorilla	70	180	Squirrel	5	13
Adult human	68	170	Mouse	2	5
White-tailed deer	65	170	Pygmy shrew	$1\frac{1}{2}$	3

Which mammals are short? medium-length? tall?

Create a length range for each category.

Short mammals are _____ inches to _____ inches in length.

Medium-length mammals are _____ inches to _____ inches in length.

Tall mammals are _____ inches to _____ inches in length.

Which two mammal lengths in the table are directly above and below your height?

Between a _____ and a _____.

According to your categories, this makes you a _____ mammal.

Use with Lesson 96.

Mammal Lengths, Part 2

How do you compare with the tallest mammal?

How many fourth graders would have to stand on each other's heads to about equal the length of a giraffe?

_____

How do you compare with the shortest mammal?

How many pygmy shrews would have to stand on each other's heads to be about as tall as a fourth grader?

_____

Compare your height with the lengths of the tallest and shortest mammals in the table.

_____

_____

_____

How many times taller are you than the shortest mammal? _____

How many times taller than you is the tallest mammal? _____

Use with Lesson 96.

Date _____ Time _____

Mammal Weights, Part 1

How does your weight compare with the weight of other mammals?

If you know your weight, write it below. Otherwise, use the weight of a "typical fourth grader" from the table below.

Weight: _____ pounds   or   _____ kilograms.

How heavy are other mammals?

Typical Weights					
Mammal	pounds	kilograms	Mammal	pounds	kilograms
Blue whale	300,000	140,000	Adult human	150	70
African elephant	12,000	5,400	Fourth grader	65	30
Giraffe	2,400	1,100	Raccoon	25	10
Bison	1,800	810	House cat	10	5
Arabian camel	1,200	540	Domestic rabbit	3	1.5
Zebra	650	290	Squirrel	1	0.5
Tiger	500	230	Mouse	0.25	0.1
Mountain gorilla	450	200	Pygmy shrew	0.01	0.005
White-tailed deer	400	180			

Source (for nonhumans): Bartoli, Stefania and Luigi Boitani. *Simon and Schuster's Guide to Mammals.* New York: Simon and Schuster, 1983.

Weight Comparison:

      A medium-size car weighs about 2,500 pounds.

      A large bus weighs about 26,000 pounds.

Which mammals are light? medium-weight? heavy?

Create a weight range for each category.

Light mammals weigh   _____ pounds to _____ pounds.

Medium-weight mammals weigh   _____ pounds to _____ pounds.

Heavy mammals weigh   _____ pounds to_____ pounds.

Are fourth graders among the light,
medium-weight, or heavy mammals? _____

Date _____ Time _____

Mammal Weights, Part 2

How does a fourth grader's weight compare with the weight of mammals of similar length?

For each of the following mammals, tell about how many fourth graders it would take to equal the length and weight of the mammal. Use inches and pounds.

	Length (in fourth graders)	Weight (in fourth graders)
Zebra	about	about
Mountain gorilla	about	about
Tiger	about	about

Further Exploration

What feature of your human shape might explain why you weigh so much less than mammals of similar length?

_____

Challenge

How does the range in mammal lengths compare with the range in mammal weights?

In the data tables on pages 228 and 230, find the tallest and shortest mammals, as well as the heaviest and lightest mammals. Write the lengths and weights in the table below. Then estimate the range of the data—that is, the difference between the largest and smallest measures. There are several ways this can be done.

	Largest	Smallest	Difference
Length			
Weight			

Which has the greater difference—length or weight? _____

Use with Lesson 96.

Math Boxes

1. The Newtons won 21 out of 43 games during last year's basketball season. The Spartans won 37 out of 78.

   Which team had the higher winning percent? _____

   What was each team's winning percent?

   Newtons _____%

   Spartans _____%

2. Sara measured the height of her classroom ceiling. Circle the most reasonable height:

   (a) 5 meters

   (b) 2 meters

   (c) 20 meters

3. Solve. Do not use a calculator.

   409 * 6 = _____

   66 * 13 = _____

4. Fill in the missing numbers on the number lines.

   a.
   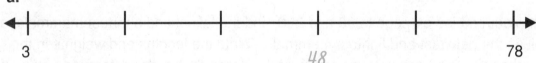
   3   ___   ___   *48*   ___   78

   b.

   7   ___   ___   ___   ___   57

Interval Estimates

Sometimes it's not possible to estimate with only one number. The value being estimated may change, or there may not be enough information. Sometimes a range of possible values is more useful than one estimated value.

An **interval estimate** is an estimate in terms of two numbers that the exact value is "between." Here is one way to give an interval estimate:

> Name a number you are sure is **less than the exact value**.

> Name another number you are sure is **greater than the exact value**.

An interval estimate can be stated in various ways.

Examples: There are at least 30 [12's] in 400, but not more than 40 [12's].

> Attendance at the game was estimated at between 90,000 and 100,000 people.

> The number of books in the school library is greater than 2000 but less than 2500.

> Between 125 and 200 people live in my building.

The smaller the difference between the upper and lower numbers, the more useful an interval estimate is likely to be.

Try a few interval estimates with your partner.

Situation	Interval Estimate

Use with Lesson 97.

Mammal Species

One of the major achievements of science is a system for classifying plants and animals. It was developed by Carolus Linnaeus (pronounced "luh KNEE us") over 200 years ago. It is still in use today. In this system, a group of animals that are similar in form and reproduce together is called a **species**. (The plural of *species* is *species*.)

Carolus Linnaeus's Classification System

	Bear	Rhinoceros
Kingdom	Animalia	Animalia
Phylum	Chordata	Chordata
Class	Mammalia	Mammalia
Order	Carnivora	Perissodactyla
Family	Ursidae	Rhinocerotidae
Genus and Species	Ursus arctos (Brown bear), Ursus americanus (Nearctic black bear), Thalarcotos maritimus (Polar bear), Selenarctos thibetanus (Asian black bear), Helarctos maylayanus (Sun bear), Melursus ursinus (Sloth bear), Tremarctos ornatus (Spectacled bear)	Rhinoceros unicornis (Indian rhino), Rhinoceros sondaicus (Javan rhino), Dicerorhinus sumatrensis (Sumatran rhino), Diceros bicornis (Black rhino), Ceratotherium simum (White or Square-lipped rhino)

Scientists have identified over 4000 species of mammals. According to this system, jackrabbits of the northern plains form one species. Snowshoe hares of the western mountains form another.

Species that share a number of features are grouped into **genera** (plural of *genus*) and genera are grouped into **families**.

There are 44 different rabbit and hare species. Each species has some unique feature that makes it different from all other species in the rabbit and hare family.

Number of Species in the Family

Koala	1	Dolphin	32
Elephant	2	Deer	34
White whale	3	Rabbit & Hare	44
Great ape	4	Kangaroo & Wallaby	50
Rhinoceros	5	Opossum	75
Porpoise	6	Monkey	127
Bear	7	Shrew	246
Pig	9	Squirrel	267
Hedgehog & Moonrat	17	Bat	950
Armadillo	20	Mouse & Rat	1082

Source (for nonhumans): Bartoli, Stefania and Luigi Boitani. *Simon and Schuster's Guide to Mammals.* New York: Simon and Schuster, 1983.

Use with Lesson 97.

Using a Division Algorithm

Here is a division algorithm you learned in class for solving 185 / 8.

```
  8)185          10      Write your estimate.
     80                  Write 10 * 8.
    105          10      Subtract.  Write your estimate.
     80                  Write 10 * 8.
     25           3      Subtract.  Write your estimate.
     24          ___     Write 3 * 8.
      1          23      Subtract.  Add the estimates.
```

The quotient is 23. The remainder is 1.

Now practice these problems using the algorithm (or one of your own).

1. 4)91 _____   2. 147 / 9 _____   3. 255 / 11 _____

4. Mrs. Jackson buys a television set for $455. She pays $100
    down and agrees to pay the remaining amount in 12 monthly
    payments. About how much will she pay each month?   _____

Use with Lesson 97.

Date _____ Time _____

Using a Division Algorithm (continued)

Make up two number stories that can be solved by division. Solve them using a division algorithm. Show your work.

5. _____

_____

_____

Solution: _____

6. _____

_____

_____

Solution: _____

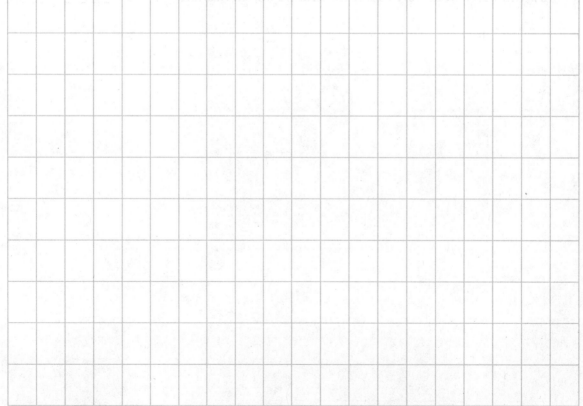

Use with Lesson 97.

Solving Multiplication and Division Number Stories

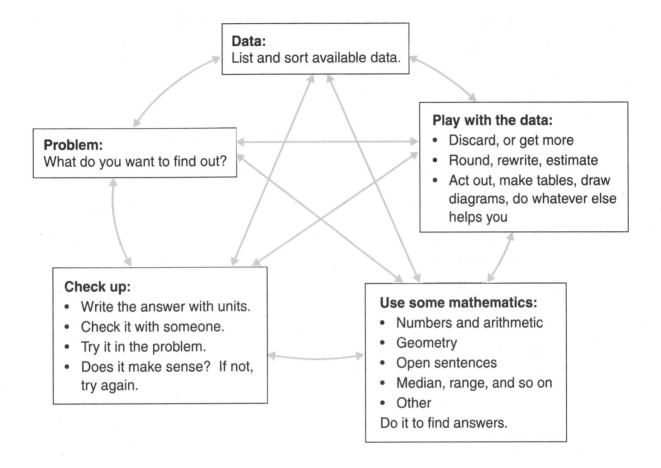

1. The profit from the used book sale at Lincoln School was $725. The Computer Club and four other clubs will share this amount equally. What is each club's share?

   Estimate. Will the solution be in the

   tens? _____ hundreds? _____ thousands? _____ (Check one.)

   Number model: _____

   Solution: _____

Solving Number Stories (continued)

2. The Box and Bin Store has 475 eight-ounce drinking glasses with "Happy Birthday" on them. These will be packed in boxes of 6, which will sell for $10.98 per box. How many boxes are needed?

   Estimate. Will the solution be in the

   tens? _____   hundreds? _____   thousands? _____   (Check one.)

   Number model: _____

   Solution: _____

3. Rocky weighed about 7 pounds at birth. Now he weighs about 200 pounds. His weight now is about how many times his weight at birth?

   Estimate. Will the solution be in the

   tens? _____   hundreds? _____   thousands? _____   (Check one.)

   Number model: _____

   Solution: _____

4. The fuel tank on Lee's car holds about 16 gallons. In the city, her car can go about 24 miles per gallon of gasoline. She starts with a full tank. About how many miles can Lee travel in the city before she has to put gasoline in her car?

   Estimate. Will the solution be in the

   tens? _____   hundreds? _____   thousands? _____   (Check one.)

   Number model: _____

   Solution: _____

5. The fastest animal on two legs is not a human or other mammal but a bird—the ostrich. A scientist observed an ostrich run about 500 feet in about 7 seconds. About what was the ostrich's speed in feet per second?

   Estimate. Will the solution be in the

   tens? _____   hundreds? _____   thousands? _____   (Check one.)

   Number model: _____

   Solution: _____

Use with Lesson 98.

Writing Multiplication and Division Number Stories

The following number models could be used to help solve number stories. For each, write a number story. Then ask your partner to solve it and write the solution, including any units. At the same time, you solve your partner's story.

1. 4 * 36 = ?

Number story: _____

_____

_____

_____

Solution: _____

2. 360 / 8 = ?

Number story: _____

_____

_____

_____

Solution: _____

3. 5280 / 6 = ?

Number story: _____

_____

_____

_____

Solution: _____

Use with Lesson 98.

Writing Number Stories (continued)

Calculator Challenge

Make up a multiplication or division number story. Use big numbers or very small numbers—numbers you would want to calculate using a calculator rather than with paper and pencil. Give the problem to your partner to solve. Remember, your problem has to make sense.

_____

_____

_____

_____

_____

Solution: _____

💡 Bookin'

In one day Americans publish about 125 new books. There are about 15 new works of fiction, 8 new children's books, 20 books on sociology and economics, and 6 books on history. There are about 5 new reference books, 8 or 9 books on medicine, 9 on philosophy or psychology, 15 on science and technology, and 6 on religion. Americans buy almost 5 million books a day.

Division Dash

Materials: a calculator for each player

Number of Players: 1 or 2

How the Game is Played:

1. Each player chooses a number and enters it on the calculator.

2. Each player presses the $\sqrt{}$ key. If the number on a player's calculator display has fewer than 3 digits, the player should repeat steps 1 and 2.

3. Each player—
   Uses the final digit on the calculator screen as a 1-digit number, and
   uses the two digits before the final digit as a 2-digit number.

4. Each player finds out **how many** of the 1-digit numbers are in the 2-digit number, and records the result. (This result is the quotient. Remainders are ignored.) Players calculate mentally or on paper, not on the calculator.

5. The players press $\sqrt{}$ and repeat steps 3 and 4 until the sum of a player's quotients is 100 or more. The winner is the first player to reach at least 100.

Example: Enter 5678.

	Quotient
Press $\sqrt{}$ and get 75.352<u>5</u><u>0</u><u>5</u>	
The problem is 50 divided by 5. Find the number of 5's in 50. Record the result. (10)	10
Press $\sqrt{}$ and get 8.6805<u>8</u><u>2</u><u>1</u>	
The problem is 82 divided by 1. Find the number of 1's in 82. Record the result. (82)	82
Press $\sqrt{}$ and get 2.9462<u>8</u><u>2</u><u>8</u>	
The problem is 82 divided by 8. Find the number of 8's in 82. Record the result. (10, ignoring the remainder)	<u>10</u>
	102

If there is only one player, the object of the game is to reach 100 or more by solving the fewest number of division problems.

Use with Lesson 99.

Date _____ Time _____

Division Dash Scoreboard

Game 1		Game 2		Game 3	
Player 1	Player 2	Player 1	Player 2	Player 1	Player 2

Game 4		Game 5		Game 6	
Player 1	Player 2	Player 1	Player 2	Player 1	Player 2

Game 7		Game 8		Game 9	
Player 1	Player 2	Player 1	Player 2	Player 1	Player 2

Use with Lesson 99.

Math Boxes

1. **a.** In December, $\frac{3}{4}$ of a foot of snow fell on Wintersville. How many inches of snow is this?

_____

b. Tina's daughter will be $\frac{3}{4}$ of a year old next week. How many months is that?

_____

2. Multiply.

a. 457 ∗ 4 = _____

b. 88 ∗ 51 = _____

3. During the basketball season, Joe made 67% of his shots. Shade the grid to represent the percent of shots Joe made. Write the amount shaded in three different ways.

fraction _____

decimal _____

percent _____

4. Round 409,381,886 to the nearest—

hundred _____

ten-thousand _____

ten million _____

hundred million _____

5. Complete.

3 yd 2 ft = _____ ft

6 yd 1 ft = _____ ft

2 ft 9 in = _____ in

25 ft = _____ yd _____ ft

Use with Lesson 99.

Mammal Heart Rates

Your heart pumps blood throughout your body. The blood carries heat, nutrients, and oxygen. It also takes away waste.

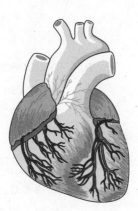

The rate at which a mammal's heart pumps is determined by the size and efficiency of the heart and by the mammal's need for heat, nutrients, and oxygen. These needs are affected by the mammal's size and amount of activity. A mammal's heart rate can tell you about the mammal's size and the kind of life it leads.

How fast does your heart beat?

If you know how, find your own heart rate; or use an estimated rate of 80 or 90 beats per minute. Record the rate below:

My heart beats about _____ times per minute.

Do you think mammals smaller than you
will have a slower or faster heart rate?   _____

Examine the chart to find out.

Mammal Heart Rate Data		
Mammal	Heartbeats per minute	Weight in pounds
Pygmy shrew	1200	0.01
Mouse	650	0.25
Guinea pig	280	0.75
House cat	110	10
Human—		
Newborn	110–160	7
7-year-old	90	50
Adult	60–80	160
Elderly	50–65	140
Tiger	40	500
African elephant	25	12,000
Gray whale	8	60,000

Source: Ontario Science Centre. *Sportworks.* Reading, MA: Addison-Wesley, 1989.

Use with Lesson 100.

Mammal Heart Rates (continued)

Do heart rate and weight seem to be related? If so, how?

_____

_____

Compare your heart rate with the rates of smaller mammals.

A mouse's heart beats about _____ times as fast as mine.

A hamster's heart beats about _____ times as fast as mine.

A house cat's heart beats about _____ times as fast as mine.

It seems as though smaller mammals have _____ (faster or slower?)
heart rates than I do.

Compare your heart rate with the rates of larger mammals.

A tiger's heart rate is about _____ (what fraction?) of mine.

An African elephant's heart rate is about _____ (what fraction?) of mine.

A gray whale's heart rate is about _____ (what fraction?) of mine.

It seems as though larger mammals have _____ (faster or slower?)
heart rates than I do.

One reason smaller mammals have faster heart rates is because they lose body
heat more quickly than larger mammals. Their hearts have to pump quickly to keep
a supply of warm blood constantly circulating throughout their bodies.

In order to create this heat, smaller mammals have to eat a lot. They tend to be more
active than larger mammals, because they are always searching for food. This puts
further demands on their heart. One result of a quicker heart rate is that smaller
mammals tend to live shorter lives. The constant activity wears them out.

Use with Lesson 100.

Mammal Heart Rates (continued)

Challenge

Could you use what you have learned to estimate a squirrel's heart rate and a bison's heart rate? Write down your ideas and discuss them with your classmates. What other information might be helpful?

_____

_____

_____

_____

_____

_____

My Estimates

I estimate that a squirrel's heart might beat about _____ times in a minute.

I think this because _____

_____

I estimate that a bison's heart might beat about _____ times in a minute.

I think this because _____

_____

See if you can find data to check your prediction.

Date _____ Time _____

Math Boxes

---

1. Complete.

50 * 60 = _____

20 * 500 = _____

400 * 80 = _____

9 * 7000 = _____

300 * 600 = _____

2. Complete.

3 pounds 21 ounces is the same

as _____ pounds 5 ounces

3 feet 21 inches is the same as

4 feet _____ inches

---

3. Solve the number sentences.

a. 2 * (6 + 1) = S S = _____

b. T / 2 = 3 + 1 T = _____

c. (R * 6) + 3 = 51 R = _____

d. Z = 24 / 12 Z = _____

4. Write 5 other names for 60%.

a. _____

b. _____

c. _____

d. _____

e. _____

---

5. 120 fourth graders attend Jason Elementary. Many of the students attend a performing arts class after school. Find the number of students for each of the following if:

a. $\frac{1}{3}$ take piano   _____

b. $\frac{1}{6}$ take acting   _____

c. $\frac{1}{8}$ take singing   _____

d. $\frac{1}{4}$ take dancing   _____

e. $\frac{1}{8}$ do not participate in a performing arts class

_____

Use with Lesson 100.

Create Your Own Mammal

New mammals are still being discovered. In dense jungles and on remote mountains, scientists are finding mammals that had never been identified before. Recently scientists found two new monkeys—a black-faced lion tamarin in the rainforests of Brazil, and a new kind of lemur on the island of Madagascar. A previously unknown antelope was observed in Vietnam.

Use your imagination to create a mammal that has never been seen before. You could combine two or three existing mammals, or think up your own.

Decide whether your mammal will be big or small. What will be its height and its length? Decide how heavy it will be and whether it will be slow or fast. Remember, the shape of its body should match its behavior and abilities. It is hard to run fast with very short legs.

1. Draw your mammal on the first sheet your teacher gives you. Fill in the blanks with information about your mammal.

2. On the second sheet your teacher gives you, fill in the blanks to tell more about your invented mammal.

Challenge

I estimate that my mammal eats about _____ pounds of food per day.

This is about _____ as many pounds as I eat.

 Is it a Bird? Is it a Mammal? Is it...

The platypus was discovered in the eighteenth century. It is an unusual animal because it has characteristics of both mammals and birds. Like birds, it lays eggs, it has a ducklike bill, and its feet are webbed. However, like mammals, the platypus nurses its young and has fur, a large brain, and claws at the end of its webbed feet. The platypus has been classified as a mammal.

Source: Louis, David. *2201 Fascinating Facts.* New York: Greenwich House, 1983.

Use with Lesson 101.

Math Message

1. Copy the distances between appliances in your kitchen from Study Link 99.

   Distance between:

   stove and sink: about _____ feet _____ inches

   sink and refrigerator: about _____ feet _____ inches

   refrigerator and stove: about _____ feet _____ inches

2. Cut out the sketch of your kitchen from Study Link 99 and tape it in the space below.

Math Message (continued)

3. Here are four ways to arrange the appliances in a kitchen.

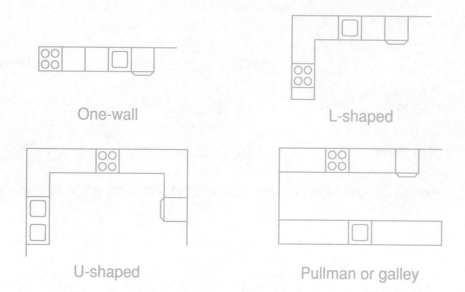

One-wall   L-shaped

U-shaped   Pullman or galley

Pullman kitchens are usually found on passenger trains. **Galleys** are the kitchens on boats and airplanes. The kitchen area on trains, boats, and airplanes is small. The cooking area is usually lined up against a single wall (a **one-wall kitchen**) or against two walls with a corridor between them (a **Pullman** or **galley** kitchen).

What kind of kitchen is your kitchen? _____

 # Two of a Kind

Excluding identical twins, what are the chances of two individuals from the same parents being exactly alike? 23 chromosomes from a mother and 23 chromosomes from a father combine to produce a new individual. Mathematically, these chromosomes can combine in over eight million ways. The chances of two individuals getting the same complement of chromosomes is about one in 70 trillion. Each chromosome may have 1250 genes. So the chances of two individuals having the same genes (identical individuals) are one in 1×10^{9031}.

Source: John Pfeiffer. *The Cell.* New York: Time-Life Books, 1964.

Use with Lesson 102.

How Efficient is Your Kitchen?

Kitchen efficiency experts are people who study the ways we use our kitchens. They carry out **time-and-motion** studies to find how long it takes to do some kitchen tasks and how much a person has to move about to do them. They want to find the best ways to arrange the stove, sink, and refrigerator. In an efficient kitchen, a person should have to do very little walking to move from one appliance to another. However, the appliances should not be too close to each other or else the person would feel cramped.

1. How well are the appliances arranged in your kitchen? With a straightedge, draw a triangle connecting the appliances in your sketch on page 249. Write the distances between the appliances next to the sides of your triangle. This triangle is called a **work triangle**.

2. Find the perimeter of your work triangle. Show your work at the right.

   Perimeter is about _____ feet _____ inches.

   That's close to _____ feet.

   _____ feet _____ inches

   _____ feet _____ inches

   + _____ feet _____ inches
   _____

   _____ feet _____ inches

3. The efficiency experts recommend the following distances between appliances:

   stove and refrigerator: 4 feet to 9 feet
   refrigerator and sink: 4 feet to 7 feet
   sink and stove: 4 feet to 6 feet

   Does your kitchen meet these recommendations? _____

4. The median work-triangle perimeter for my class is about _____ feet.

Use with Lesson 102.

Work Triangles

1. Draw a work triangle to show an arrangement of appliances that meets the following conditions:

    *   The perimeter is 21 feet.

    *   The length of each side is a whole number of feet.

    *   The length of each side is within the recommended range.

            stove and refrigerator: 4 to 9 feet
            refrigerator and sink: 4 to 7 feet
                    sink and stove: 4 to 6 feet

    Record the length of the sides on the triangle.

    Label each vertex (corner) of the triangle as "stove," "sink," or "refrigerator."

2. Draw a different work triangle that meets the same requirements listed in Part 1.

A Floor Plan of My Classroom

When designing a room or a house, architects must make very accurate drawings, called **scale drawings**. For example, if the window in a room is halfway between two ends of a wall, then the window in a scale drawing of the room must also be at the halfway point. If the wall is four times as long as the window sill, then the wall in the scale drawing must also be four times as long.

1. What information do you need to make a scale drawing of your classroom?

_____

_____

_____

_____

Architects use the following symbols to show doors and windows in their scale drawings.

window   door opening to left   door opening to right

2. Make a rough sketch of your classroom.

Use with Lesson 103.

Date _____ Time _____

A Floor Plan of My Classroom (continued)

Make a scale drawing of your classroom.

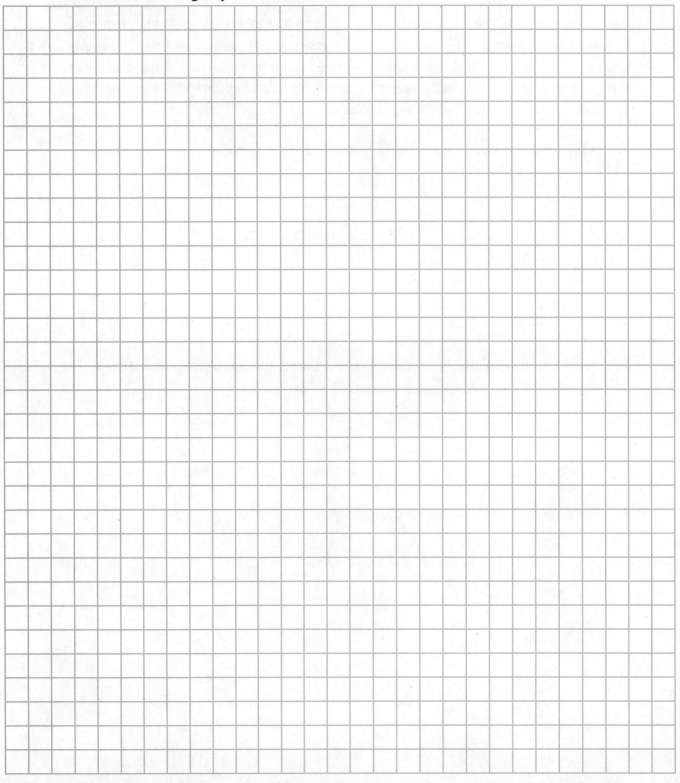

Scale: _____

For Lesson 104: The area of my classroom is about _____ square feet.

Use with Lesson 103.

Math Boxes

---

1. Write 5 other names for 75%.

    a. _____

    b. _____

    c. _____

    d. _____

    e. _____

---

2. Find a number in the *World Tour Book* with a 5 in the ten-thousands place.

_____

On what page did
you find the number? _____

Read the number to a friend.

---

3. Sally spends $\frac{1}{3}$ of the day at school. How many hours does she spend at school? (Hint: 24 hours in a day) _____

Of the amount of time Sally spends in school, $\frac{1}{4}$ of that is spent at lunch, recess, music, gym, and art. How many hours are spent at these activities? _____

---

4. Complete.

    a. 24 in = _____ ft

    b. 27 in = _____ ft _____ in

    c. 48 oz = _____ lb

    d. 54 oz = _____ lb _____ oz

    e. 72 oz = _____ lb _____ oz

---

5. Solve.

    a. 456 / 14 _____

    b. 1032 / 21 _____

Use with Lesson 103.

What is Area?

Mr. Samuel is building a large bulletin board for his classroom. He wants to cover a 4-by-6 foot rectangular piece of plywood with cork tiles. The store sells square tiles that measure 1 foot on each side. How many tiles does he need to buy to cover the whole wooden board?

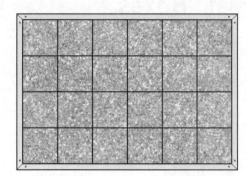

The number of tiles needed to cover the board gives the **area** of the board. Area is measured in **square units**. Each cork tile measures 1 square foot, so the area of the plywood board is 24 square feet. This measurement can also be written as *24 ft²*.

There are many situations in which you need to know the area of a surface.

- If you wanted to install wall-to-wall carpeting in your living room, you would find the area of the floor to figure out how much carpeting to buy. You would use square yards (yd²) in the U.S. and square meters (m²) elsewhere.

- The labels on cans of paint usually tell about how many square feet of surface can be painted before you need to open a new can. To estimate how many gallons of paint to buy to paint the walls and ceilings of the rooms in your home, you would find the total area of all the surfaces to be painted.

- In your *World Tour Book*, the size of each country you visit is given in square miles. This is useful when you want to compare the size of countries.

Be careful not to confuse the **area** of a shape with its **perimeter**. The area of a shape is the amount of surface *inside* the shape. The perimeter is the distance *around* the shape. Area is measured in units such as square inches, square feet, square centimeters, square meters, and square miles. Perimeter is measured in units such as inches, feet, centimeters, meters, and miles.

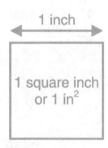

1 inch

1 square inch or 1 in²

In the next few lessons, you will solve many area problems. Later on, you will use what you know about area to investigate the furniture arrangement in your bedroom.

Use with Lesson 104.

Area of Polygons

Find the area of each polygon.

1 sq. cm

1.

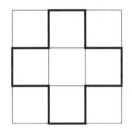

Area = _____ sq. cm

2.

Area = _____ sq. cm

3.

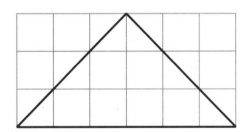

Area = _____ sq. cm

4.

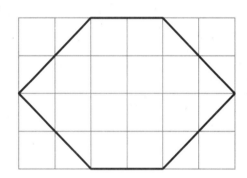

Area = _____ sq. cm

5.

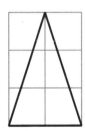

Area = _____ sq. cm

6.

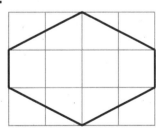

Area = _____ sq. cm

7.

Area = _____ sq. cm

Use with Lesson 104.

Math Boxes

---

1. Draw an angle that is greater than 60°, but less than 130°. Then measure and record.

_____°

2. Complete.

  a. 17 in = _____ ft _____ in

  b. 43 in = _____ ft _____ in

  c. 6 ft = _____ yd

  d. 11 ft = _____ yd _____ ft

  e. 4 yd = _____ ft

---

3. The Senior class at Rees High School raised $1897 for five local charities in the community. The money will be equally shared among the five charities. How much will each charity receive? Use a computation grid if necessary.

_____

---

4. Write the four numbers below in order from smallest to greatest.

3,000,000

one hundred thousand

2.5 billion

10^6

_____ _____ _____ _____

Use with Lesson 104.

Date _____ Time _____

Area of Rectangles

Math Message

1. Find the area of each rectangle.

1 sq. cm

A

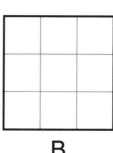
B

C

Area = _____ sq. cm   Area = _____ sq. cm   Area = _____ sq. cm

2. Fill in the table.

Rectangle	Number of squares per row	Number of rows	Total number of squares	Number model
A	4	2		
B				
C				

3. Write a formula for finding the area of a rectangle.

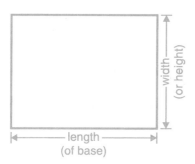

Area = _____

Use with Lesson 105.

Area of Rectangles (continued)

4. Fill in the table.

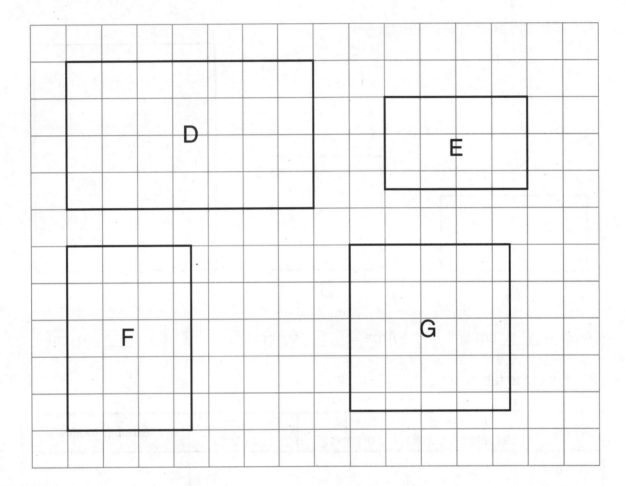

Rectangle	Area (counting squares)	Length (of base)	Width (or height)	Area (using formula)
D	_____ cm²	_____ cm	_____ cm	_____ cm²
E	_____ cm²	_____ cm	_____ cm	_____ cm²
F	_____ cm²	_____ cm	_____ cm	_____ cm²
G	_____ cm²	_____ cm	_____ cm	_____ cm²

Use with Lesson 105.

Calculator 10,000

Materials: a calculator

Object: To get from a "starting number" to 10,000 or as close as possible by using each of the four operations—addition, subtraction, multiplication, and division—once.

How to form a starting number: Pick any number from 1 to 12. **Cube** it.

> *Example:* Pick 5. Cube it: $5 * 5 * 5 = 125$
> 125 is the starting number.

One-player Game

1. Form a starting number and enter it in your calculator; for example, 125.

2. Pick a number. **Add**, **subtract**, **multiply**, or **divide** it with your starting number. Example: Pick 100. Multiply it with your starting number. $125 * 100 = 12,500$

3. Pick a different number. Add, subtract, multiply, or divide it with your result in step 2. Use a **different** operation from the one in step 2.

> *Example:* Pick 2. Divide the result in step 2 by 2. $12,500 / 2 = 6250$

4. Continue to pick numbers and do operations until you have done each of the 4 operations once. You can do the operations in any order, but do each operation only once. You must pick a different number for each operation.

Before you start, decide whether to choose numbers to add, subtract, multiply, and divide from Level 1 or Level 2.

> *Level 1:* any number except 0
> *Level 2:* only numbers from 2 to 100   Level 2 is harder.

For each game, record what you did on page 262.

Two-player Game

Players choose the level and the number of rounds in a game before the start of the game. In each round, each player gets one turn: One player chooses the starting number. The other player enters it in the calculator and tries to get as close to 10,000 as possible.

Scoring: Find the difference between your final result and 10,000 for each round. At the end of the game, find your total score. The player with the lower total score wins the game.

Use with Lesson 106.

Calculator 10,000 Score Sheet

Level 1 Games (Use any number except 0.)

Starting number	Final result	What I did
$5^3 = 125$	10,150	$125 * 100 = 12,500$ $12,500 \mid 2 = 6250$ $6250 - 3000 = 3250$ $3250 + 6900 = 10,150$

Level 2 Games (Use any number from 2 to 100.)

Starting number	Final result	What I did

Use with Lesson 106.

Math Boxes

1. Harold's Suit Store is offering a 25% discount on all regular priced suits for one week. Find the discounted price for each suit.

Regular price	Discount	Discount price
$400	$100	_____
$200	_____	_____
_____	$85	_____

2. Jill's little sister will be exactly $1\frac{1}{2}$ years old on Monday. How many months old is she?

   _____ months

   Joe bought a door that is $6\frac{1}{2}$ feet tall. How many inches is this?

   _____ inches

3. Solve.

   a. 490 / 7   _____

   b. 1024 / 11   _____

4. Write each number using digits. Then round each number to the nearest thousand.

   a. twenty million, one hundred fifty-two thousand, six hundred twenty-five

   number: _____   rounded: _____

   b. three hundred twelve thousand, eight hundred fifty

   number: _____   rounded: _____

Use with Lesson 106.

What is the Area of My Skin?

Trace your hand on the grid below.

What Is the Area of My Skin? (continued)

Follow your teacher's directions to complete this page.

1. There are _____ square inches in 1 square foot.

2. My guess is that the area of my skin is about _____ square feet.

Rule of thumb: The area of a person's skin is about 100 times the area of the outline of that person's hand.

Use this rule of thumb to estimate the area of your skin.

- First, ask your partner to trace the outline of your hand on the grid on page 264.

- Estimate the area of the tracing of your hand by counting squares. Record your estimate in Part 3 below.

- Use the rule of thumb to estimate the area of your skin (area of hand * 100). Record your estimate in Part 4 below.

3. I estimate that the area of the tracing of my hand is about _____ square inches.

4. I estimate that the area of my skin is about _____ square inches.

5. I estimate that the area of my skin is about _____ square feet.

6. There are _____ square feet in 1 square yard.
   I estimate that the area of my skin is about _____ square yards.

---

7. Find the area of these polygons.

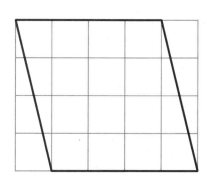

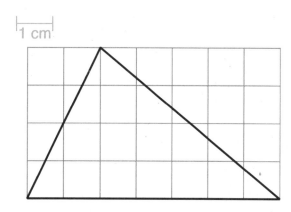

Area = _____ cm²   Area = _____ cm²

Use with Lesson 107.

Math Boxes

---

1. Write a number story for the number sentence 756 / 12 = *x*. Then solve the problem.

_____

_____

_____

_____

Answer: _____

---

2. Round the following numbers to the nearest ten-thousand.

a. 150,983 _____

b. 786,042 _____

c. 12,903,899 _____

d. 79,067,409 _____

3. Complete.

a. 100 cm = _____ m

b. 1000 cm = _____ m

c. 345 cm = _____ m _____ cm

d. 5 m = _____ cm

e. 6.7 m = _____ cm

---

4. A number has

6 in the tenths place

9 in the hundreds place

0 in the thousands place

7 in the ones place

3 in the tens place

5 in the hundredths place

Write the number.

_____

Round the number to the nearest tenth.

_____

Geographical Area Measurements

You may remember that the heights of mountains and depths of oceans are obtained *directly*, by measuring the earth itself. The areas of countries and oceans are found *indirectly*—by measuring very accurate maps or satellite pictures instead of the countries and oceans themselves.

Countries, oceans, and deserts have irregular boundaries. To measure their areas, you can use a method that is similar to the one you used to find the area of Manhattan Island: Place a transparent grid of squares on a map and count the squares and parts of squares that cover the region you are measuring. The squares should be drawn to the same scale as the map.

There are a number of reasons why it is difficult to make very accurate area measurements of such regions.

Area of a country Because there may not be agreement on the exact boundary of a country, area measurements may vary depending on which boundary is used.

Area of a lake, sea, or ocean Some bodies of water are bounded by shoreline on all sides. Because the shoreline varies depending on the level of the water, it is almost impossible to get a very accurate measurement of the area covered by water.

It is even more difficult to determine the areas of the world's oceans because they are not separated from one another by shorelines. As with the boundaries of countries, there may not be agreement on the location of the boundary lines between oceans.

Area of a desert This measurement is especially difficult to make because desert boundaries may vary as a result of changes in the climate or because of cultivation of the land. Also, there is no agreement on what constitutes a desert. Some geologists define a desert as land that is not suitable for agriculture, others define it as land that supports neither agriculture nor grazing. Then there are deserts that are hot and dry only part of the year, depending on the season. Others are dry year-round, either because it is very hot or, in very cold climates, because the water is always frozen. The very cold deserts are known as **tundras**.

Use with Lesson 108.

Date _____ Time _____

Math Boxes

1. Measure ∠ABC and ∠DEF.

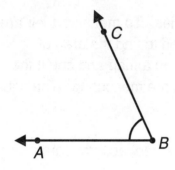

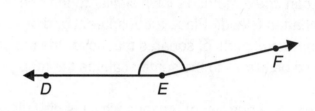

∠ABC = _____ °   ∠DEF = _____ °

---

2. Divide.

   a. 982 / 9   _____

   b. 909 / 11   _____

---

3. Using a line of symmetry draw the other half of the drawing.

---

4. I am a four-digit number.

   • The digit in the ones place is a 1.

   • The value of the tens digit is 3 more than that of the ones digit.

   • The value of the hundreds digit is 5 more than that of the ones digit.

   • The value of the thousands digit is 7 more than that of the ones digit.

   What number am I? _____

---

5. Complete.

   a. 1000 mm = _____ m

   b. 2200 mm = _____ m _____ cm

   c. 5 m = _____ mm

   d. 3.8 m = _____ m _____ cm

   e. 15.3 m = _____ m _____ cm

Use with Lesson 108.

Area of Parallelograms

1. Cut out shape A on Activity Sheet 20. Do not cut out the shapes on this page.

Parallelogram A	Tape your rectangle in the space below.
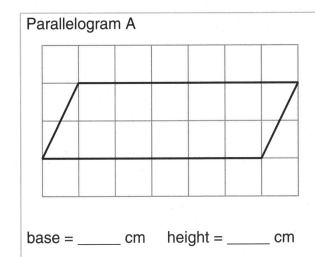	
base = _____ cm height = _____ cm	length = _____ cm width = _____ cm
Area of parallelogram = _____ sq. cm	Area of rectangle = _____ sq. cm

2. Do the same with shape B on your Activity Sheet.

Parallelogram B	Tape your rectangle in the space below.
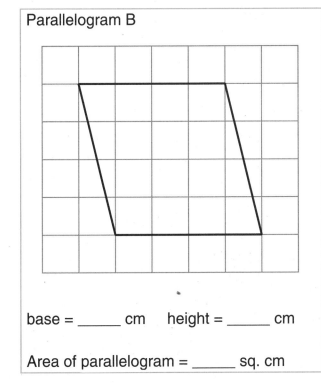	
base = _____ cm height = _____ cm	length = _____ cm width = _____ cm
Area of parallelogram = _____ sq. cm	Area of rectangle = _____ sq. cm

Use with Lesson 109.

Area of Parallelograms (continued)

3. Do the same with shape C.

Parallelogram C	Tape your rectangle in the space below.
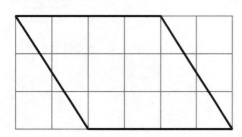	
base = _____ cm height = _____ cm	length = _____ cm width = _____ cm
Area of parallelogram = _____ sq. cm	Area of rectangle = _____ sq. cm

4. Do the same with shape D.

Parallelogram D	Tape your rectangle in the space below.
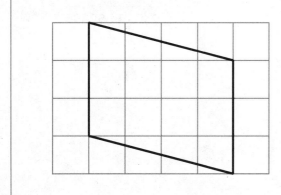	
base = _____ cm height = _____ cm	length = _____ cm width = _____ cm
Area of parallelogram = _____ sq. cm	Area of rectangle = _____ sq. cm

5. Write a formula for finding the area
of a parallelogram.

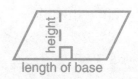

_____

Area of Parallelograms (continued)

1. Measure the base and height of parallelogram *DORA*.

   What is the area of the parallelogram?

   length of base = _____ cm

   height = _____ cm

   Area = _____ sq. cm

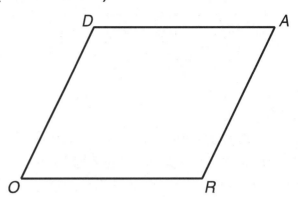

2. Draw the following shapes on the grid below.

   a. A rectangle whose area is 12 square centimeters.

   b. A parallelogram that is not a rectangle whose area is 12 square centimeters.

   c. A different parallelogram whose area is also 12 square centimeters.

3. What is the area of:

   a. parallelogram *ABCD*?   **b.** trapezoid *EBCD*?   **c.** triangle *ABE*?

   _____ cm²   _____ cm²   _____ cm²

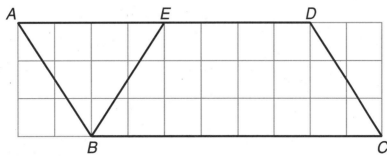

Use with Lesson 109.

Constructing a Parallelogram

Step 1: Draw an angle *ABC*.

Step 2: Set one point of the compass at *B* and the other at *C*. Without changing your compass opening, place your compass point on point *A* and draw an arc.

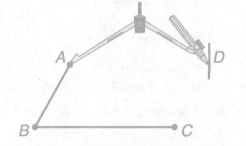

Step 3: Set one point of the compass at *B* and the other at *A*. Without changing your compass opening, place your compass point on point *C* and draw another arc that crosses the first arc. Label the point where the two arcs cross point *D*.

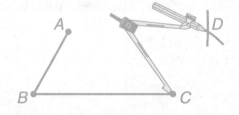

Step 4: Draw line segments *AD* and *CD*.

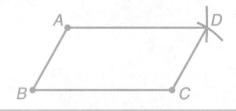

Construct a parallelogram in the space below.

Date _____ Time _____

Constructing a Line Segment Perpendicular to Another Line Segment from a Point *on* the Line Segment

Line segments that meet at right angles are **perpendicular** to each other.

Step 1: Draw line segment *AB*. Make a dot on $\overline{AB}$ and label it point *P*.

Step 2: Place your compass point on point *P*, and draw an arc that crosses $\overline{AB}$ at point *C*. Keeping your compass point on point *P* and the same compass opening, draw another arc that crosses $\overline{AB}$ at point *D*.

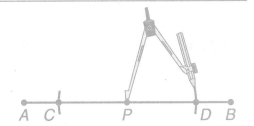

Step 3: Place your compass point on point *C*, make the compass opening larger than $\overline{CP}$, and draw an arc above $\overline{AB}$. Keeping the same compass opening, place your compass point on point *D* and draw another arc above $\overline{AB}$ that crosses the first arc. Label the point where the two arcs cross point *Q*.

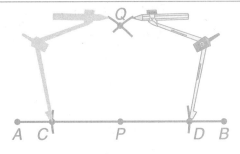

Step 4: Then draw $\overline{QP}$.

$\overline{QP}$ is **perpendicular** to $\overline{AB}$.

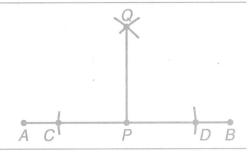

1. Construct a line segment perpendicular to $\overline{FX}$ to point *R*.

Use with Lesson 109.

Constructing a Line Segment Perpendicular to Another Line Segment from a Point *not on* the Line Segment

Step 1: Make a dot and label it point *M*. Draw $\overline{PQ}$ below point *M*.

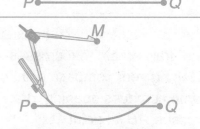

Step 2: Place your compass point on point *M* and draw an arc that crosses $\overline{PQ}$ at two points.

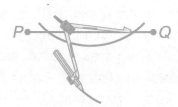

Step 3: Place your compass point on one of the points and draw an arc below $\overline{PQ}$.

Step 4: Keeping the same compass opening, place your compass point on the other point and draw another arc that crosses the first arc. Label the point where the two arcs cross point *N*. Then draw $\overline{MN}$.

$\overline{MN}$ is **perpendicular** to $\overline{PQ}$.

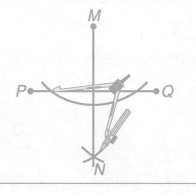

1. Construct a line segment from point *G* perpendicular to $\overline{HI}$.

   G

2. On your construction of the parallelogram on page 272, construct a line segment to show the height of the parallelogram.

H ●————————————————● *I*

Area of Triangles

1.   Cut out triangles A and B from Activity Sheet 21. Do not cut out the one below.
     Tape the triangles together to form a parallelogram.

Triangle A	Tape your parallelogram in the space below.
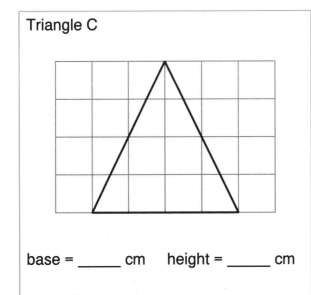	
base = _____ cm height = _____ cm	base = _____ cm height = _____ cm
Area of triangle = _____ sq. cm	Area of parallelogram = _____ sq. cm

2.   Do the same with triangles C and D.

Triangle C	Tape your parallelogram in the space below.
base = _____ cm height = _____ cm	base = _____ cm height = _____ cm
Area of triangle = _____ sq. cm	Area of parallelogram = _____ sq. cm

Use with Lesson 110.

Area of Triangles (continued)

3. Do the same with triangles E and F.

Triangle E	Tape your parallelogram in the space below.
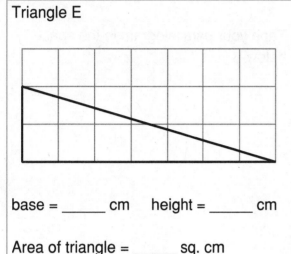	
base = _____ cm height = _____ cm	base = _____ cm height = _____ cm
Area of triangle = _____ sq. cm	Area of parallelogram = _____ sq. cm

4. Do the same with triangles G and H.

Triangle G	Tape your parallelogram in the space below.
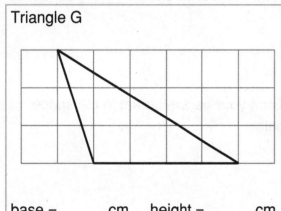	
base = _____ cm height = _____ cm	base = _____ cm height = _____ cm
Area of triangle = _____ sq. cm	Area of parallelogram = _____ sq. cm

5. Write a formula for finding the area of a triangle.

_____

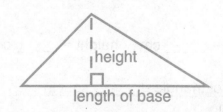

Area of Triangles (continued)

1. Measure the base and height of
    triangle *SAM*. Find the area.

    base = _____ cm   height = _____ cm

    Area = _____ sq. cm

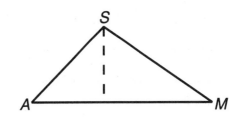

2. Draw three different triangles on the grid below, each with an area of 3 square
    centimeters. One of the triangles should be a right triangle.

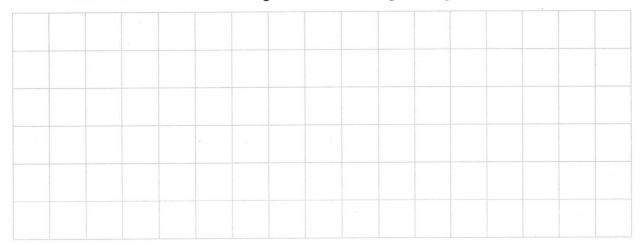

Challenge

3. Which has the larger area–the star or the square? Explain your answer.

    _____

    _____

    _____

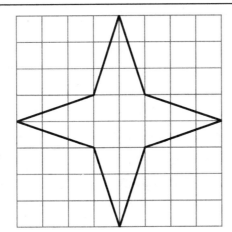

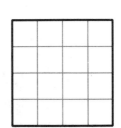

Use with Lesson 110.

My Bedroom Furniture

1. Use the scale drawings of your bedroom and bedroom furniture to complete the tables below. Round the measurements to appropriate units.

	Length	Width	Area
bedroom floor			

Furniture	Length	Width	Area

2. What is the total area of the furniture? about _____ sq. _____

3. What fraction of your bedroom floor is taken up by furniture? _____

4. What percent of your bedroom floor is taken up by furniture? _____

5. What is the median percent for the class? _____

6. You might want to arrange your bedroom furniture in a different way. If so, move the furniture on your scale drawing first to make sure it will fit. When you are sure of the way you want to arrange it, ask someone at home to help you move it.

Use with Lesson 111.

Date _____ Time _____

Math Boxes

1. Fill in the missing values that represent the amount that is shaded.

   a.

   b. $\dfrac{\Box}{100}$

   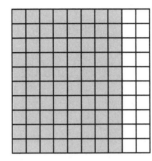

   c. 0._____   d. _____ %

2. The Sports Boosters raised $907 at their annual chili supper. The money will be shared equally by 4 different athletic teams. How much money will each team receive? Use a computation grid if necessary.

   a. Will the solution be in the— tens? hundreds? thousands? (Circle one)

   b. Number model: _____

   c. Solution: _____

3. Continue the counts.

   −15, −10, −5, _____, _____, _____

   0.02, 0.12, 0.22, _____, _____, _____

   25, 15, 5, _____, _____, _____

   0.34, 0.41, 0.48, _____, _____, _____

4. Shananda measured herself and found she was 51 inches tall. Two years ago she was 4 feet tall. How much had she grown in two years?

   _____

Use with Lesson 111.

Date _____ Time _____

Math Message

1 pint = _____ cups

1 quart = _____ pints

1 half-gallon = _____ quarts

1 gallon = _____ quarts

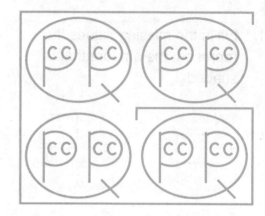

How can the picture above help you remember how many cups are in a pint, how many pints are in a quart, and how many quarts are in a gallon?

Rice Consumption

1. Round your answer to the nearest ounce:
    One cup of dry (uncooked) rice weighs about _____ ounces.

2. Use the answer in Part 1 to complete the following.

    a. 1 pint of rice weighs about _____ ounces.

    b. 1 quart of rice weighs about _____ ounces.

    c. 1 gallon of rice weighs about _____ ounces.

    d. 1 gallon of rice weighs about _____ pounds. (1 pound = 16 ounces)

3. On an average, a family of 4 in Japan eats about 40 pounds of rice a month. That's about how many pounds a year?   _____

    How many gallons?   _____

4. On an average, a family of 4 in the U.S. eats about 88 pounds of rice a year. That's about how many gallons a year?   _____

5. On an average, a family of 4 in Thailand eats about 3 gallons of rice a week. That's about how many **gallons** a year?   _____

    How many **pounds**?   _____

Use with Lessons 112 and 113.

Date _____ Time _____

Math Boxes

---

1. Fill in the missing values.

	fraction	decimal	percent
a.	_____	_____	75%
b.	_____	1.00	_____
c.	$\frac{4}{5}$	_____	_____
d.	_____	_____	30%

---

2. 27 fourth-grade students collected newspapers for one week. If they collected a total of 2078 newspapers throughout the week, about how many papers did each student collect?

a. Will the solution be in the— tens? hundreds? thousands? (Circle one)

b. Number model: _____

c. Solution: _____

---

3. a. Which is warmer,
−15°C or −3°C? _____

b. How many degrees
warmer? _____

c. Which is colder,
−15°C or −20°C? _____

d. How many degrees
colder? _____

4. I am a four-digit number greater than 9000.

- The digit in the ones place is 3.
- The digit in the hundreds place is 7.
- The sum of the four digits is 20.

What number am I?

_____

Use with Lesson 113.

Date _____ Time _____

Rates

1. A typical student in my class blinks _____ times in one minute while at rest.

2. A typical student in my class blinks _____ times in one minute while reading.

3. List as many examples of rates as you can.

   _____

   _____

   _____

   _____

   _____

   _____

   _____

   _____

   _____

4. Find at least 2 examples of rates in your *World Tour Book*.

   _____

   _____

   _____

   _____

Use with Lesson 115.

Math Boxes

1. Multiply.

    a. 509 * 6 _____

    b. 237 * 9 _____

2. Complete.

    a. 22 c = _____ gal _____ pt

    b. 5 gal = _____ qt

    c. 8 qt 3 pt = _____ c

    d. 1 gal 6 qt = _____ pt

    e. 3 qt 16 c = _____ gal

3. Write a number story for 593 / 12. Then solve the problem.

_____

_____

_____

_____

_____

Answer: _____

4. Fill in the missing numbers.

Rule : $\frac{1}{2}$ of

in	out
6	*3*
_____	20
$\frac{1}{2}$	_____
_____	$\frac{4}{4}$

5.

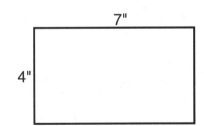

Area = _____sq. inches

Rates

For each problem, fill in the rate table. Then answer the question below the table.

1. Bill's new car can travel about 35 miles on 1 gallon of gasoline.

Gasoline mileage: 35 miles per gallon

miles	35							
gallons	1	2	3	4	5	6	7	8

At this rate, about how far can the car travel on 7 gallons of gas?_____ miles

2. Jennifer received an allowance of $8.00 in 4 weeks.

Allowance: $8 in 4 weeks

allowance			$8.00					
weeks	1	2	3	4	5	6	7	8

At this rate, how much allowance did she receive per week? $ _____

3. A gray whale's heart beats 24 times in 3 minutes.

Whale's heart rate: 24 beats in 3 minutes

heartbeats			24					
minutes	1	2	3	4	5	6	7	8

At this rate, how many times did the
gray whale's heart beat in 2 minutes?   _____ times

4. Mr. Johnson paid $1.80 for 3 pounds of grapes.

Cost of grapes: $1.80 for 3 pounds

pounds	1	2	3	4	5	6	7	8
cost								

At this rate, how much would 5 pounds of grapes cost? $ _____

Use with Lesson 116.

Date _____ Time _____

Math Message

It is estimated that the average lifetime of a person living in the United States is about 75 years.

About how many days are there in an average lifetime?   about _____ days

About how many hours is that?   about _____ hours

Do These Numbers Make Sense?

1. It is estimated that in an average lifetime, a person sleeps about 214,000 hours. At that rate, about how many hours per day does a person sleep?*   _____ hours per day

   Does this number make sense to you? _____

2. It is estimated that in an average lifetime of 75 years, a person watches TV about 105,000 hours. At that rate, about how many hours per day does a person watch TV?*   _____ hours per day

   Does this number make sense to you? _____

3. It is estimated that in an average lifetime of 75 years, a person laughs about 540,000 times. At that rate, about how many times a day does a person laugh?*   _____ times per day

   Does this number make sense to you? _____

4. It is estimated that in an average lifetime, a person takes about 95,000,000 breaths. Does this number make sense to you? Explain.

   _____

   _____

   _____

*Source: McCutcheon, Marc. *The Compass in your Nose and Other Astonishing Facts about Humans.* Los Angeles: Jeremy P. Tarcher, Inc. 1989.

Use with Lesson 117.

Math Boxes

1. Write 5 other names for $\frac{6}{8}$.

    a. _____

    b. _____

    c. _____

    d. _____

    e. _____

2. Measure the length and width of your journal to the nearest half inch. Find its perimeter.

length = _____ inches

width = _____ inches

perimeter = _____ inches

3. This recipe makes 8 cups of lemonade: 5 lemons + $\frac{3}{4}$ cup sugar + $\frac{1}{2}$ gallon water.

    a. How much water would you need for 4 cups of lemonade? _____

    b. How many lemons would you need for 24 cups of lemonade? _____

4. Name a percent value greater than $\frac{1}{5}$ and less than $\frac{1}{2}$.

    _____

5. If the average person eats about 20 cups of popcorn per month, about how many quarts of popcorn would that equal? (Hint: 1 quart equals 4 cups)

    _____ quarts

6. Write <, >, or =.

    a. 28 + 32 _____ 44 + 16

    b. 10 + 20 + 30 _____ 25 + 45

    c. 18 + 33 _____ 35 + 14

    d. 120 − 12 _____ 110 + 2

    e. 12 ∗ 2 _____ 48 / 2

Use with Lesson 117.

Date _____ Time _____

Math Boxes

1. Right now it is about

    _____ minutes after _____ o'clock,

    or _____:_____.

    Half an hour ago it was

    _____:_____.

    In 25 minutes it will be

    _____:_____.

2. If you throw one die 60 times, how many times would you expect

    to come up?

    _____

3. Divide.

    a. 504 / 8 _____   b. 2045 / 11 _____

4. Complete.

    a. 2 pt = _____ qt

    b. 12 qt = _____ gal

    c. 8 c = _____ gal

    d. 20 c = _____ gal _____ pt

    e. 5 gal = _____ qt

5. What is the area of the parallelogram? ($A = b * h$)

    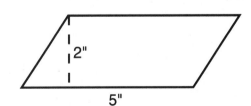

    area = _____ sq. in

Use with Lesson 118.

Math Message: Product Testing

Some magazines written for young people, such as *Zillions*, employ their readers to test many different kinds of products. The results of the tests are then published in the magazines to help their readers make wise buying decisions. For example, in one issue, 44 of the magazine's readers taste-tested several brands of potato chips. They considered taste, cost, and nutritional value as they tried to decide which brand was the "best buy." In another issue, a team of testers compared 37 brands of peanut butter in their search for the best product.

When a reader wrote to the magazine to complain about a board game she had bought, the magazine sent board games to young people in every part of the country. Testers were asked to play each game several times and report on what they liked and disliked about the game.

1. If you were testing a board game, what are some of the features you would look for?

   _____

   _____

   _____

2. When the readers of the magazine tested potato chips, they considered taste, cost, and nutritional value in determining the best chip. Which of these is the most important to you?

   _____

   _____

   _____

3. What is a **consumer**? Be prepared to share your definition with the class.

   _____

   _____

   _____

   _____

Use with Lesson 119.

Math Boxes

---

1. Multiply.

    a. 349 * 4 _____   **b.** 240 * 18 _____

---

2. Fill in the missing numbers.

a.

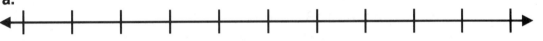

0   *1*   *3.5*   5

___ ___ ___ ___ ___ ___ ___ ___ ___

b.

0   20

___ ___ ___ ___ ___ ___ ___ ___ ___

---

3. Complete.

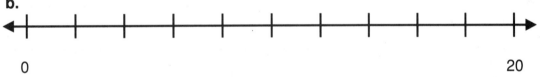

	fraction	decimal	percent
a.	$\frac{1}{2}$	_____	_____
b.	_____	0.20	_____
c.	$\frac{1}{10}$	_____	_____
d.	_____	_____	40%

Math Message: Which is the Better Buy?

1. A store sells a certain brand of cereal in two sizes.

- a 10-ounce box that costs $2.50

- a 15-ounce box that costs $3.60

Which size box is the better buy? _____

Why? _____

_____

_____

2. Suppose you can buy a box of 16 crayons for 80 cents or a box of 32 crayons of the same kind for $1.28. Which is the better buy? _____

Why? _____

_____

_____

3. A store sells a 4-pack of AA batteries for $2.40 and a 6-pack of the same kind for $3.30. Which is the better buy? _____

Why? _____

_____

_____

Unit Pricing

Round the answers in Problems 1–3 to the nearest tenth of a cent.

1. A 15-ounce bottle of shampoo costs $3.89. What is
   the price per ounce?   _____

2. Two pounds of sliced turkey from the deli cost $9.78.
   What is the price per ounce?   _____

3. A package of 6 candy bars costs $2.89. At this rate,
   what is the price of 1 candy bar?   _____

4. A 6-ounce bag of potato chips costs $1.50. A 14-ounce bag costs the same
   amount per ounce as the 6-ounce bag. How much does the 14-ounce bag cost?
   Explain your answer.

   _____

   _____

   _____

   Which is the better buy—the 6-ounce bag or the 14-ounce bag? _____

Challenge

5. A store sells a 3-pound can of coffee for $7.98 and a 2-pound can of the same
   brand for $5.98. You can use a coupon worth 70 cents toward the purchase of
   the 2-pound can. If you used the coupon, which would be the better buy, the
   3-pound can or the 2-pound can? Explain your answer.

   _____

   _____

   _____

   _____

Use with Lesson 120.

Which Soft Drink Would You Buy?

For each set of soft-drink containers, record the following information:

- The name of the place from which the containers come
- The size of the container (small, medium, or large)
- The price
- The capacity in fluid ounces

Then calculate the unit price in cents per fluid ounce, rounded to the nearest tenth of a cent.

Soft-drink containers from:			
Size	Price	Capacity (fl. oz)	Unit price (¢/fl. oz)

Soft-drink containers from:			
Size	Price	Capacity (fl. oz)	Unit price (¢/fl. oz)

Soft-drink containers from:			
Size	Price	Capacity (fl. oz)	Unit price (¢/fl. oz)

Use with Lesson 121.

Math Boxes

1. Draw a rectangle whose area is 12 square centimeters and whose perimeter is 16 centimeters.

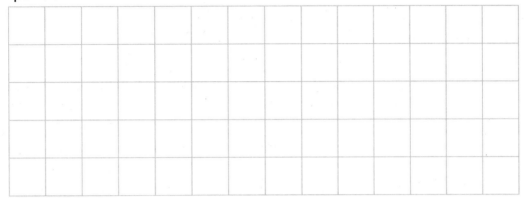

2. Complete.

   a. 3 pints = _____ cups

   b. 2 quarts 1 pint = _____ cups

   c. 1 gallon = _____ cups

   d. 5 pints = _____ cups

   e. 2 gallons 1 pint = _____ cups

3. Divide.

   a. 4981 / 14   _____

   b. 544 / 8   _____

4. Lewis Elementary had a fund-raiser to buy more books for the school library. The fourth-grade class set a goal for each student to collect at least $25. If each student reaches that goal, how much money will a class of 33 fourth graders collect for the fund-raiser?

   a. Will the solution be in the— tens?   hundreds?   thousands?   (Circle one)

   b. Number model: _____

   c. Solution: _____

Use with Lesson 121.

2-Dimensional and 3-Dimensional Figures

A **polygon** is a 2-dimensional figure made up of line segments joined at their endpoints. A rectangle is a polygon with four sides and four right angles.

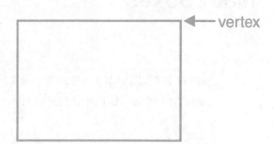

A point where two sides of a polygon meet is called a **vertex** of the polygon.

All of the points in a polygon lie in one **plane**, or flat surface.

A circle is the set of all the points in a plane that are the same distance (the radius) from a point called the **center** of the circle. A circle is not a polygon.

The points of the plane inside a polygon or circle make up its interior. The **area** of a plane figure is a measure of its interior.

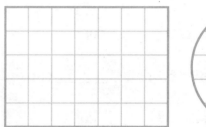

A **geometric solid** is a 3-dimensional shape made up of surfaces. The surfaces can be curved or flat. The points of a geometric solid do not all lie in the same plane.

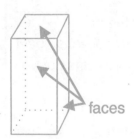

The surfaces of some geometric solids are formed by polygons. These flat surfaces are called **faces** of the solid. The rectangular prism at the left has 6 faces.

Many cardboard boxes are good models of rectangular prisms. The sides are the faces.

A cylinder has 3 surfaces: a flat "top" and a flat "bottom" formed by circles, and the curved surface that connects them.

A food can is a good model of a cylinder.

2-Dimensional and 3-Dimensional Figures (continued)

Like a circle, a sphere is the set of all the points that are the same distance from a point called the **center**. But these are points in space, not just in one plane.

A basketball or world globe is a good model of a sphere.

The surfaces of a geometric solid meet in curves or line segments. These curves or line segments are called **edges** of the solid.

As with polygons, a "corner" of a geometric solid is called a **vertex** (plural *vertexes* or *vertices*). Edges meet at a vertex.

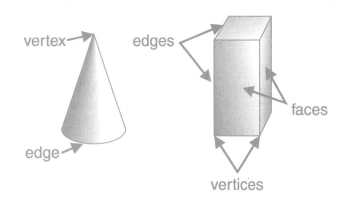

1. A rectangular prism has _____ faces.

2. A rectangular prism has _____ edges and _____ vertices.

The measure of the space inside a closed 3-dimensional geometric shape is called **volume** (rather than area).

 # Waterlogged?

The earth weighs 6,588,000,000,000,000,000,000,000 tons and travels through space at a speed of 660,000 miles per hour. If the world were to become totally flat and the oceans distributed themselves evenly over the earth's surface, the water would be approximately 2 miles deep at every point.

Source: Louis, David. *2201 Fascinating Facts*. New York: Greenwich House, 1983.

Use with Lesson 123.

Date _____ Time _____

Modeling a Rectangular Prism

After you make your rectangular prism, answer the following questions.

1. How many faces does your rectangular prism have? _____

2. How many of these faces are formed by rectangles? _____

3. Are any faces formed by squares? If so, how many? _____

4. Pick an edge. How many other edges are parallel to it? _____

5. Pick one of the faces. How many other faces are parallel to it? _____

6. Write T (true) or F (false) for each of the following statements about the rectangular prism you made.

    _____ I have no curved surfaces.

    _____ I am a cylinder.

    _____ All of my faces are formed by polygons.

    _____ I have exactly four faces.

    _____ I have more vertices than faces.

    _____ All of my edges are parallel.

7. Draw a picture of your rectangular prism below. You can show hidden edges with dashed lines (- - - - - -).

Math Boxes

1. Gum costs $0.80 per pack. How much will it cost to buy—

   4 packs of gum? _____

   10 packs of gum? _____

   16 packs of gum? _____

2. Build a numeral. Write:

   2 in the tens place
   8 in the hundred thousands place
   5 in the millions place
   3 in the tenths place
   7 in the hundreds place
   9 in the ones place
   4 in the thousands place
   1 in the ten thousands place

   _____

3. **a.** I am thinking of a number. If I multiply it by 9 the answer is 90.

   What is the number? _____

   b. I am thinking of a number. If I divide it by 6, the answer is 8.

   What is the number? _____

4. What is the value of the 7 digit in the numbers below?

   a. 474 _____

   b. 70,158 _____

   c. 187,943 _____

   d. 2,731,008 _____

5. Estimate the height of your chair. Now measure it.

   Estimate:

   about _____ _____ (unit)

   Measurement:

   about _____ _____ (unit)

6. In each of the following, write a number that makes the sentence true.

   a. 4 * _____ > 29

   b. 48 / _____ < 24

   c. 9 * _____ < 62

   d. 24 / _____ > 10

Use with Lesson 123.

Geometric Solids

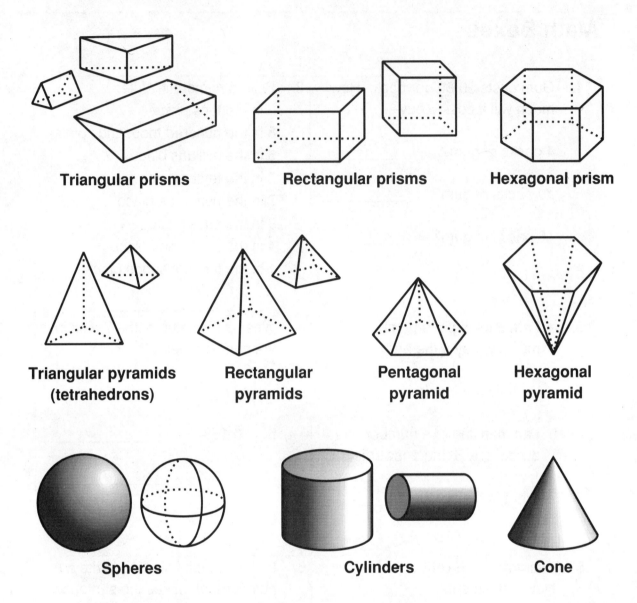

Triangular prisms   **Rectangular prisms**   **Hexagonal prism**

**Triangular pyramids
(tetrahedrons)**   **Rectangular
pyramids**   **Pentagonal
pyramid**   **Hexagonal
pyramid**

Spheres   **Cylinders**   **Cone**

Five regular polyhedrons The faces that make each shape are identical.

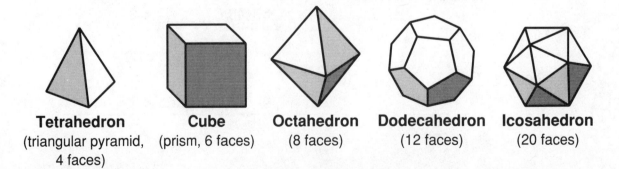

Tetrahedron
(triangular pyramid,
4 faces)

Cube
(prism, 6 faces)

Octahedron
(8 faces)

Dodecahedron
(12 faces)

Icosahedron
(20 faces)

Use with Lesson 124.

Math Message: Riddles

Find the following geometric solids on page 298.

1. I have 6 faces. All faces are rectangles. Who am I? _____

2. I have the same number of faces as vertices.
Who am I?   _____

3. I have only one surface. It is curved. I have no
base. Who am I?   _____

Activity: Construction of Polyhedrons

Polyhedrons are geometric solids with all flat surfaces. Use your straws and connectors to make each of the following polyhedrons. Then answer the questions about them. Look at page 298 to help you with the shapes and their names.

4. I am a polyhedron.
I have 5 faces.
4 of my faces are formed by triangles.
One of my faces is a square.

   a. After you make me, draw a picture of me.

   b. Who am I?   _____

   c. How many corners (vertices) do I have?   _____

   d. What shape is my base?   _____

5. I am a polyhedron.
I have 4 faces.
All of my faces are formed by equilateral triangles.
All of my faces are the same size.

   a. After you make me, draw a picture of me.

   b. Who am I?   _____

   c. How many vertices (corners) do I have?   _____

   d. What shape is my base?   _____

Use with Lesson 124.

Math Boxes

1. Draw a quadrangle that does not have any right angles.

What kind of quadrangle is this?

_____

2. Write 5 names for 1000.

a. _____

b. _____

c. _____

d. _____

e. _____

3. Two cups of flour are needed to make about 20 medium-sized peanut butter cookies. How many cups of flour will you need to make—

40 cookies? _____

60 cookies? _____

50 cookies? _____

4. Give at least 3 other names for each measure.

1 gal _____ _____ _____

1 qt _____ _____ _____

1 pt _____ _____ _____

5. Complete the table.

number of pizzas	1	2		4	5	6
number of servings	3		9	12		

How many pizzas are needed for 21 servings? _____

6. Solve.

a. 3953 / 8 _____

b. 8723 / 5 _____

Making a Model of a Tetrahedron

In a **regular** geometric solid, all the edges are the same length. The following directions tell how to make a model of a regular triangular pyramid, or **regular tetrahedron**. Each face is formed by an equilateral triangle.

1. Cut out four circles with equilateral triangles from the "Circle and Equilateral Triangle Patterns."

Step 1

2. Fold each paper along the sides of the triangle.

Step 2

3. Lay down one of your paper circles and unfold it so that the three curved flaps stick up. It will be the base.

4. Take another paper circle. Match a side of its triangle with a side of the triangle on the base. Use staples, tape, or glue to fasten the two curved flaps together.

Steps 3 and 4

5. In the same way, attach the other two paper circles to other sides of the base.

Step 5

6. Fold up the three paper circles that you attached to the base. The triangles come together to form the tetrahedron. You can push all the flaps inside and tape the edges together. Or leave two or three flaps outside and tape or glue them to the tetrahedron.

Step 6

Finished

 ## Structurally Sound?

When 15 years old, John Sain set a record for building a house of cards with the greatest number of stories. His tower reached 12 feet and 10 inches and had 68 stories.

Source: *The Guinness Book of Records 1993.* New York: Facts On File, 1992.

Use with Lesson 125.

Making a Model of a Tetrahedron (continued)

Look at the regular triangular pyramid, or regular tetrahedron, that you constructed.

1. Describe the faces using geometric terms.

    _____

    _____

2. Which does your tetrahedron have
    more of: faces, edges, or vertices?   _____

3. Draw a picture of your tetrahedron below. Try to make it look 3-dimensional.

4. Put your partner's tetrahedron together with yours to form a new geometric solid.

    How many faces does it have?   _____

    Draw it below.

Math Boxes

1. Draw a square that has a perimeter of 16 cm.

What is the area of the square?

_____ _____
                (unit)

2. Write a number story for the number sentence 806 / 12. Then solve the problem.

_____

_____

_____

_____

Answer: _____

3. Show three ways to divide a square into four equal parts.

4. Draw a line segment that is 2 inches long. Mark and label every $\frac{1}{4}$ of an inch.

Date _____ Time _____

Building Structures

1. Use the blueprint at the right to build a structure on the Blueprint Mat. Use centimeter cubes.

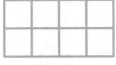

	back		
2	1	1	0
0	0	0	0
1	2	0	1
0	1	1	0

left side / right side

front

   a. Compare your structure with the structure built by your partner. They should look the same.

   b. Draw all four views of your structure by shading squares.

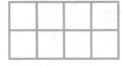

front view   left-side view   back view   right-side view

   c. Compare your views with those drawn by your partner. They should be the same.

2. Build any structure you wish on your Blueprint Mat. Reminder: Use no more than 2 cm cubes on a square.

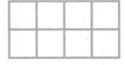

back

left side / right side

front

   a. Record your structure on the blueprint at the right.

   b. Draw all four views of your structure by shading squares.

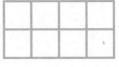

front view   left-side view   back view   right-side view

   Ask your partner to check your work.

   c. Compare the views of opposite sides of your structure.

3. Here is the front view of a structure. Draw its back view.

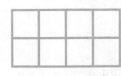

front view   back view

Use with Lesson 126.

Date _____ Time _____

More Structures

Math Message: Here are two views of a structure. Draw its other two views.

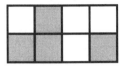 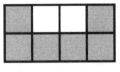 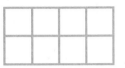 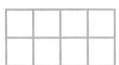

front view   left-side view   back view   right-side view

1. Here are the front view and the left-side view of a structure.

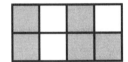 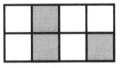

front view   left-side view

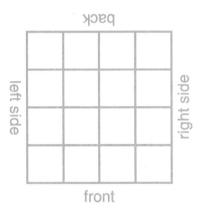

    a. Build a structure that has these views.
         Record it on the blueprint at the right.

    b. Compare your structure and blueprint with
         your partner's. Are they the same?   _____

2. Work with your partner. Use the following front view and left-side view to build
    3 different structures. Record each structure on one of the blueprints.

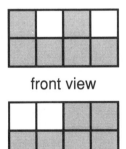 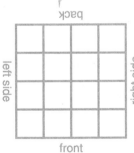 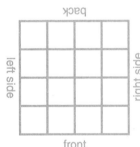 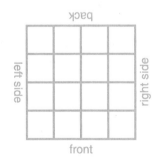

front view

left-side view

3. **a.** Is it possible to build two different structures from the
         same front and left-side views?   _____

    b. Is it possible to build two different structures from the
         same front, left-side, back, and right-side views?   _____

Use with Lesson 127.

Math Boxes

---

1. Round 5,906,245 to the—

nearest million _____

nearest ten thousand _____

nearest thousand _____

---

2. Multiply.

a. 785 * 6 = _____

b. 1034 * 9 = _____

---

3. Following is the data for the number of days it took 10 students to complete their science projects:

6, 4, 10, 11, 8, 6, 14, 9, 3, 12

What is the range for this set of numbers? _____

What is the median? _____

---

4. During a schoolwide clean-up, each student was to pick up at least 10 pieces of garbage. If there are 583 students at this school, about how many pieces of trash in all should they pick up?

_____

---

5. Draw the following angles. Use a protractor.

    a. $\angle EDF = 78°$

    b. $\angle NMO = 121°$

Use with Lesson 127.

Advanced Credits/Debits

Materials: 1 deck of playing cards or *Everything Math Deck*
1 penny with red dot on the tails side
recording sheet (page 308)

Number of players: 2

Red Alerts:

Pretend that you are an accountant for a new business. Your job is to keep track of the company's "bottom line." You will do this by recording the debits and credits which are reported to you.

Because this is a new business, the accounting system is not perfected yet. At times, credits or debits are reported incorrectly. You are informed of such errors by a notice called a "Red Alert." When you receive a "Red Alert," you must subtract the incorrect debit or credit from the bottom line.

Directions:

1. Shuffle the deck and lay it face down between you and your partner.

2. The black cards are the "credits" and the blue or red cards are the "debits."

3. The heads side of the coin tells you to add a credit or debit to the bottom line. The red side of the coin signals a "Red Alert." You must subtract a credit or debit from the bottom line.

4. Each player begins with a bottom line of $10.

5. Take turns. When it is your turn:
    *   Flip the coin. This tells you whether to add or subtract.
    *   Draw a card. This tells you what amount (positive or negative) to add or subtract from the bottom line.
    *   Record the result on page 308.

6. After 10 turns or at the end of the playing time, whichever comes first, the partner in the best financial position wins the round.

Use with Lesson 128.

Date _____ Time _____

Advanced Credits/Debits Recording Sheet

		Game 1		
	Start	**Change**		**End, and next start**
		Addition or Subtraction	Credit or Debit	
1	+$10			
2				
3				
4				
5				
6				
7				
8				
9				
10				

		Game 2		
	Start	**Change**		**End, and next start**
		Addition or Subtraction	Credit or Debit	
1	+$10			
2				
3				
4				
5				
6				
7				
8				
9				
10				

Use with Lesson 128.

Math Boxes

1. A 10-oz can of fruit costs $0.79. A 16-oz can of fruit costs $1.49. Which can of fruit is the better buy? _____

What is the price per ounce for each can? (Round to the nearest tenth of a cent.)

10 oz _____

16 oz _____

2. Change the following fractions to percents (you may want to use your calculator).

a. $\frac{3}{4}$ = _____ %

b. $\frac{3}{5}$ = _____ %

c. $\frac{12}{40}$ = _____ %

3. Fill in the missing values on the number lines below.

a.

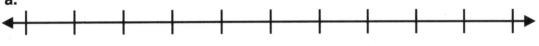

0   *1*   2

_____ _____ _____ _____ _____ _____ _____ _____ _____

b.

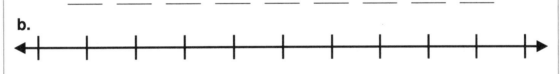

5   *6.5*   10

_____ _____ _____ _____ _____ _____ _____ _____ _____

4. Solve.

a. _____ = 109 − 48

b. 409 = _____ + 285

c. _____ − 678 = 930

d. 377 + _____ = 1000

e. 735 = _____ + 397

5. You drive at an average speed of 50 miles per hour. How far do you get in—

a. 3 hours?   _____

b. $\frac{1}{2}$ hour?   _____

c. $2\frac{1}{2}$ hours?   _____

d. 12 hours?   _____

Use with Lesson 129.

What is Volume?

The **volume** of a solid object, such as a brick or a ball, is the measure of how much space the object takes up. The volume of a container, such as a freezer, is the measure of how much the container will hold. The volume of containers that are usually filled with a liquid, such as a gasoline tank, is often called its **capacity**.

It is easy to find the volume of objects that are shaped like cubes or other rectangular prisms. For example, you might try this: On a sheet of paper, draw a pattern for an open box. The bottom of the box should be a rectangle 4 centimeters long and 3 centimeters wide. The box should be 2 centimeters high. (You can use centimeter grid paper or dot paper to help you draw the pattern.) Cut out the pattern and tape it together. Then fill the box with centimeter cubes. The number of cubes needed to fill the box is the volume of the box.

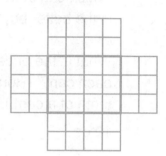

Volume is measured in **cubic units**. There are 12 cubes in 1 layer in the box you constructed, so there are 24 cubes in 2 layers. Therefore, the volume of the box is 24 cubic centimeters, or 24 cm^3.

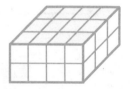

Notice that all you need to know to find the volume of a box are its linear **dimensions**—the length and width of its base and its height. Later on, you will learn how to find the volume of other solids, such as triangular prisms, pyramids, cones, and spheres, by measuring their dimensions. It is even possible to find the volume of irregular objects, such as rocks or your own body.

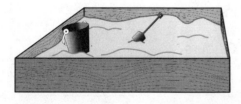

The volume of an object can be very useful to know. For example, suppose you wanted to buy sand to fill a sandbox. To estimate how much sand to buy, measure the dimensions of the empty sandbox and use these dimensions to calculate how many cubic feet (or cubic yards) of sand to order. You could do similar calculations to determine how much concrete is needed to build a patio or how much gravel to buy for a path in the backyard.

What is Volume?

Use your dictionary to find as many different meanings of the word **volume** as you can.

Write each definition below. For each definition, write a sentence containing the word *volume*.

Meaning of *volume*   Sentence that uses the word *volume*

1. _____   _____

_____   _____

_____   _____

_____

2. _____   _____

_____   _____

_____   _____

_____

3. _____   _____

_____   _____

_____   _____

_____

4. _____   _____

_____   _____

_____   _____

_____

Use with Lesson 130.

Cube Stacking Problems

Imagine that each picture at the bottom of this page and on the next page shows a box, partially filled with cubes. The cubes in each box are the same size. Each box has at least one stack of cubes that goes all the way up to the top.

Your task is to find the number of cubes needed to completely fill each box.

Record your answers in the table below.

	Box 1	Box 2	Box 3	Box 4	Box 5	Box 6
Number of cubes needed to cover the bottom						
Number of cubes in the tallest stack*						
Number of cubes needed to fill the box						

* Be sure to count the bottom cube.

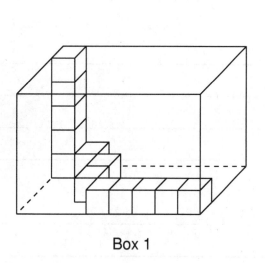

Box 1

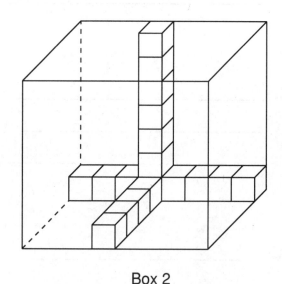

Box 2

Cube Stacking Problems (continued)

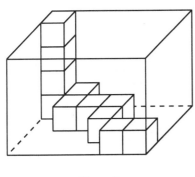

Box 3

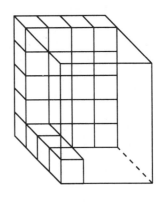

Box 4

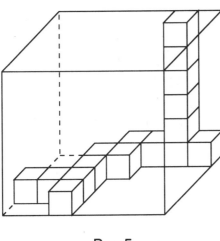

Box 5

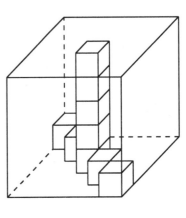

Box 6

Formula for the volume of rectangular prisms:

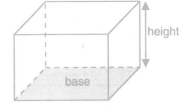

_____

B is the **area** of a base.

h is the height from that base.

Volume units are cubic units.

Use with Lesson 131.

Cube Stacking Problems (continued)

Find the volume of each of the following stacks of cm cubes.

1.

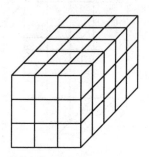

Volume = _____ cm³

2.

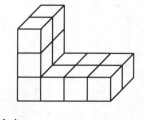

Volume = _____ cm³

3.

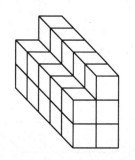

Volume = _____ cm³

4.

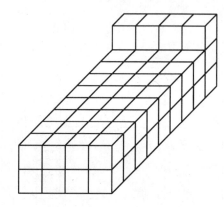

Volume = _____ cm³

5.

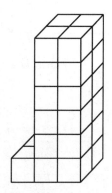

Volume = _____ cm³

6.

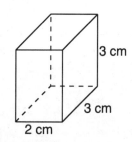

Volume = _____ cm³

 # One Cubic Foot

If you have trouble imagining how large a cubic foot is, use two large brown paper grocery bags to make one. Cut off the top of each bag to a height of 12 inches.

The bottom of each bag is about 1 foot long and about $\frac{1}{2}$-foot wide. So, if you open them and place them side by side, they have a volume of about 1 cubic foot.

Use with Lesson 131.

Building Prisms

1. Use cm cubes to build the prism
    shown as shaded on the
    3-dimensional grid.

    Volume = _____ cm^3

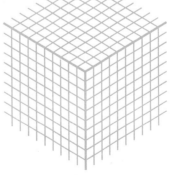

2. Build a different prism that has the
    same volume as the prism in Part 1.
    Shade the grid to show the prism.
    Record the results in the table on
    page 316.

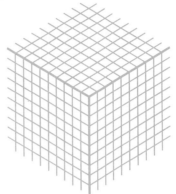

Use your cm cubes to build the following rectangular prisms. Then shade the grids
to show the prisms you built. Record the results in the table on page 316.

3. Build a prism that has a volume of
    36 cm^3 and a height of 3 cm.

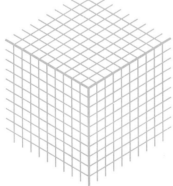

4. Build a prism that has a volume of
    36 cm^3 and a height of 6 cm.

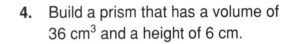

5. Build a prism that has a volume of
    36 cm^3 and a 2-cm square base.

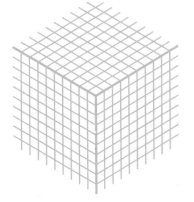

6. Build a prism that has a volume of
    27 cm^3.

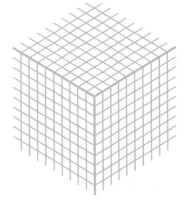

Use with Lesson 131.

Building Prisms (continued)

Record the results from page 315 in the table below.

Prism	Length of base	Width of base	Height of prism	Volume
1	6cm	2cm	2cm	24cm³
2				
3				
4				
5				
6				

 # What is the Volume of...

A sheet of paper: Believe it or not, a sheet of paper has volume.

You can estimate the volume of a single sheet by cutting and measuring. Suppose that you cut a sheet of notebook paper into 1-inch squares and then stack them into a neat pile. Your pile of squares would be about $\frac{1}{4}$-inch high.

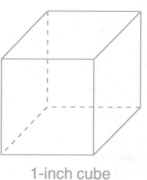

1-inch cube

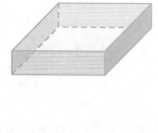

What would be the volume of a single sheet of paper?   about _____ in³

Your body: To figure out the volume of your body, you can use this rule of thumb:

Every 60 pounds of body weight has a volume of about 1 cubic foot.

What is the volume of your body?   about _____ ft³

Use with Lesson 131.

A Record Rainfall

Math Message: According to the National
Weather Service, the most rain that fell in the
United States in a 24-hour period was 42 inches.
This record rainfall took place in Alvin, Texas, on
July 25 and 26, 1979.

Imagine that it rained 42 inches in your
classroom. About how many pounds would the rainwater weigh?

Think about how you would solve this problem.

• What information do you need?

• How would you find this information?

• How would you use this information to solve the problem?

Jot down some of your ideas.

_____

_____

_____

_____

_____

_____

_____

 There is a saying...

"A pint's a pound the world around."

Here's why. A cubic foot of water has a capacity of a little less than 8 gallons.
8 gallons is 32 quarts, or 64 pints.
Therefore, 64 pints of water weighs a little more than 62.5 pounds, and
1 pint weighs about 1 pound.

Use with Lesson 132.

Date _____ Time _____

A Record Rainfall (continued)

> 1 cubic foot of rainwater
> weighs about 62.5 pounds.

Work with your group to solve the problem.

1. About how many pounds would the
   rainwater in your classroom weigh?   about _____ lb

   How many tons?   about _____ tons

2. What information did you use to solve the problem? How did you find this
   information?

   _____

   _____

   _____

   _____

3. Describe what you did to solve the problem.

   _____

   _____

   _____

   _____

   _____

   _____

   _____

Math Boxes

1. Write 8,042,176 using words.

_____

_____

_____

_____

2. Make true sentences by inserting parentheses.

a. 7 * 4 − 4 = 0

b. 45 / 9 + 10 = 15

c. 8 * 7 − 6 = 8

d. 24 / 3 + 5 = 13

3. Shade in 0.6 of the grid at the right.

Write the value shaded as a:

decimal _____

fraction _____

percent _____

How much more would need to be shaded to get to 0.9? _____

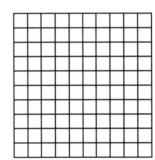

4. Tell if each of these is closer to a millimeter (mm), a centimeter (cm), a decimeter (1 dm = 10 cm), or a meter (m).

a. width of a pencil _____

b. width of a doorway _____

c. thickness of thread _____

d. length of your calculator _____

5. Jake can ride his bike 5 miles in 40 minutes. At this rate how long does it take him to ride 1 mile?

_____

Date _____   Time _____

Maya Numerals

Write each Maya numeral with digits.

1. _____

 = 4 [20's] = _____

 = 13 [1's] = + _____

_____

_____

2. _____

━━━━━

━━━━━

• (over line)

3. _____

• (over line)

• • •

• (over line)

4. _____

• •

━━━━━━ (double line)

•

• • •

Challenge

5. Write each base-10 numeral as a Maya numeral.

   a. 153   **b.** 1594

Math Boxes

1. Using your ruler, draw a line segment that is 6 inches long. Mark points that are the following distances from the left end of the line segment: $\frac{9}{16}$", $1\frac{5}{8}$", $3\frac{1}{2}$", $4\frac{3}{16}$", $5\frac{1}{8}$", and $5\frac{15}{16}$". Compare your results with a friend.

2. Find the solution of each open sentence. Write a number sentence with the solution in place of the variable.

Open Sentence	Solution	Number Sentence
$y = 6 * 12$	_____	_____
$9 = 81 / a$	_____	_____
$98 + s = 425$	_____	_____
$a = 708 - 292$	_____	_____

3. Carlos, Frank, Mia, and Lauren each have a different favorite fruit: apples, grapes, watermelons, or peaches.

   • Carlos likes a fruit that has a large seed in it.

   • Mia likes a smaller fruit that is usually green or red.

   • Lauren does not like watermelon or grapes.

   What fruit is the favorite of each student?

   Lauren _____   Carlos _____

   Frank _____   Mia _____

Use with Lesson 133.

Date _____ Time _____

Coming Home

It is time to complete the World Tour.

1. Fly to Washington, D.C., and then travel to your hometown.

    In your *Student Record Book*:

    a. Mark the final leg of the tour on the Route Map on page 22.

    b. Complete your Route Log on page 2.

2. What is the total distance you have traveled?   _____ miles

3. The airline has given you a coupon for every
    5000 miles you have traveled. Pretend that you did
    all your traveling by plane on the same airline. How
    many coupons have you earned on the World Tour?   _____ coupons

4. You can trade in 5 coupons for one free round-trip
    ticket to fly anywhere in the continental United
    States. How many round-trip tickets have you
    earned on the World Tour?   _____ round-trip tickets

Looking Back

Refer to the Country Diaries in your *Student Record Book* as you answer the
following questions.

1. What are some things you have enjoyed on the World Tour?

    _____

    _____

    _____

    _____

Use with Lesson 134.

Looking Back (continued)

2. What are some things about the World Tour you did not enjoy?

   _____

   _____

   _____

3. If you could travel all over the world for a whole year, what information would you need in order to plan your trip?

   _____

   _____

   _____

   _____

4. To which country would you most like to travel in your lifetime? Tell why.

   _____

   _____

   _____

5. On your travels, you would have the opportunity to learn about many different cultures. What would you want to share with people from other countries about your culture?

   _____

   _____

   _____

   _____

Use with Lesson 134.

Date _____ Time _____

Math Boxes

---

1. Write 5 other names for $\frac{4}{5}$.

   a. _____

   b. _____

   c. _____

   d. _____

   e. _____

---

2. You burn up about 60 calories playing tennis for 10 minutes. How many minutes must you play tennis to burn up 300 calories? Fill in the table.

calories	60		180	240	300
minutes	10	20	30		

---

3. Solve.

   a. 34 * 69 = _____

   b. 473 * 9 = _____

---

4. Write a missing equivalent fraction or decimal.

        Decimal   Fraction

   a.   .40   _____

   b.   _____ $\frac{3}{4}$

   c.   _____ $\frac{6}{6}$

   d.   0.3   _____

---

5. Find the missing numbers and rule.

       Rule: _____

in	out
9	63
10	____
5	____
4	28

---

6. If 4 shirts cost $80.00, how much for:

   3 shirts? _____

   6 shirts? _____

Glossary

acute angle An angle that measures less than 90°.

angle A figure consisting of two *rays* with the same *endpoint*.

area The measure of the surface inside a closed boundary.

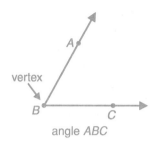

angle *ABC*

bank balance The amount of money in a bank account at a given time.

bar graph A graph that uses horizontal or vertical bars to represent data.

base-ten system A system for writing numbers based on groupings in tens, hundreds, thousands, and so on.

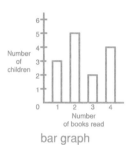

bar graph

base of a parallelogram One of the sides of a parallelogram. The shortest distance between the base and the side opposite the base is the *height* of the parallelogram.

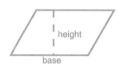

base of a triangle One of the sides of a triangle. The shortest distance between the *base* and the *vertex* opposite the base is the *height* of the triangle.

capacity A measure of how much liquid a container can hold.

census A survey taken by the government of a country. It includes a count of the population and other information helpful in planning the kinds of services the government needs to provide.

center of a circle A point that is the same distance from all points on a circle.

centimeter (cm) In the metric system, a unit of length defined as $\frac{1}{100}$ of a meter; equal to 10 millimeters, or $\frac{1}{10}$ of a decimeter.

circle The set of all points in a plane that are the same distance from a given point (the *center* of the circle).

circumference The distance around a circle.

clockwise rotation A rotation in the direction of the rotation of the hands of a clock.

circle

concave polygons

concentric circles

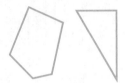

convex polygons

cube

concave polygon A polygon in which at least one vertex is "pushed in." Also called *nonconvex*.

concentric circles Circles that have the same center.

convex polygon A polygon in which all vertices are "pushed out."

counterclockwise rotation A rotation in the opposite direction of the rotation of the hands of a clock.

credit An amount, such as a deposit, added to a bank balance.

cube A polyhedron with six faces, each formed by a square.

cube (of a number) The product of a number used as a factor three times. For example, the cube of 5 is 5 ∗ 5 ∗ 5, or 125.

cubic unit A unit used in a volume measurement.

data Numerical and other factual information that may be derived from scientific experiments, surveys, or in other ways that rely on observation, questioning, and measurement.

debit An amount, such as a withdrawal, subtracted from a bank balance.

degree (°) A unit of measure for angles; based on dividing a circle into 360 equal parts.

denominator The number of equal parts into which the whole (the unit or the ONE) is divided. In the fraction $\frac{a}{b}$, b is the denominator.

deposit An amount of money, put into a bank account, that is added to the *bank balance*.

diameter A line segment that passes through the center of a circle or sphere and has its endpoints on the circle or sphere; also, the length of such a segment.

digit In our base-ten numeration system, one of the symbols 0, 1, 2, 3, 4, 5, 6, 7, 8, 9. For example, the numeral 145 is made up of the digits 1, 4, and 5.

dimension A measure in one direction.

discount The amount by which the *regular price* of an item on sale is reduced.

dodecahedron A polyhedron with twelve faces. (See *regular polyhedron*.)

endpoint The point at either end of a line segment; also, the point at the beginning of a ray. A line segment is named by its endpoints: "Segment *LT*" or "segment *TL*" is the line segment between (and including) points *L* and *T*.

equally likely Events that have the same chance of occurring.

equilateral triangle A triangle with all three sides the same length.

equivalent fractions Fractions that name the same number.

estimate A "rough" calculation; not exact.

exponent See *exponential notation.*

exponential notation A notation used to represent the *power of a number.* For example, $5^3 = 5 * 5 * 5$ represents the third power of 5. The raised 3 is called the *exponent*; it tells the number of times 5 is used as a factor.

extended multiplication fact A product of tens, hundreds, thousands, and so on, in which all but the first digit of each factor are zeros (for example, $6 * 70$, $60 * 7$, $60 * 70$).

fact family A group of related multiplication and division facts: $6 * 7 = 42$, $7 * 6 = 42$, $42/6 = 7$, $42/7 = 6$.

factor A number that is being multiplied. In $4 * 3 = 12$, 4 and 3 are factors and 12 is the *product.*

formula A general rule for finding the value of something. A formula is often written in abbreviated form with letters, called *variables.* For example, the formula for the area of a parallelogram, can be written as $A = b * h$ where the letter *A* stands for the area, the letter *b* for the length of the base, and the letter *h* for the height of the parallelogram.

frieze pattern A design made by repeating one or more shapes along a strip by *reflections, rotations*, and/or *translations (slides).*

geometric solid A 3-dimensional shape bounded by surfaces. Common geometric solids include the rectangular prism, square pyramid, cylinder, cone, and sphere. A geometric solid is "hollow;" it does not include the points in its interior.

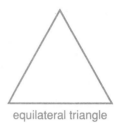

equilateral triangle

5^{3} ←exponent

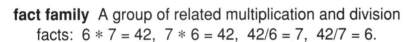

$4 * 3 = 12$

factors   product

heptagon

hexagon

hexagram

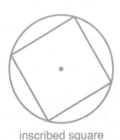

inscribed square

kite

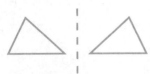

line of reflection

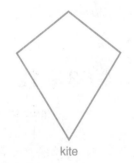

line of symmetry

height of a parallelogram See *base of a parallelogram.*

height of a triangle See *base of a triangle.*

hemisphere One half of a sphere.

heptagon A polygon with seven sides.

hexagon A polygon with six sides.

hexagram A six-pointed star formed by extending the sides of a regular hexagon.

icosahedron A polyhedron with twenty faces. (See *regular polyhedron.*)

image The reflection of a picture or object that you see when you look through a transparent mirror.

inscribed polygon A polygon whose vertices are points on a circle or other figure.

interest An amount earned for the use of money deposited in a savings account. The *rate of interest* (usually given as a percent naming cents per dollar) is used to calculate the amount of interest earned.

interior The set of all points of the plane "inside" a closed 2-dimensional figure such as a polygon or circle, or all points of space "inside" a closed 3-dimensional figure such as a polyhedron or sphere. The interior is usually not considered to be part of the figure.

intersect To meet.

kite A quadrilateral with two pairs of adjacent equal sides.

landmarks Measures, used to describe a set of data, including *median, mean, mode, maximum, minimum,* and *range.*

latitude The measure of an angle, whose vertex is the center of the earth, used to indicate the location of a place with reference to the equator.

line (straight line) A geometric figure that can be thought of as a line segment that extends in both directions without end.

line of reflection (mirror line) A line halfway between a picture or object *(pre-image)* and its reflected *image.*

line of symmetry A line of reflection in the middle of a picture or object.

line plot A "rough" graph used to display the number of times each value in a set of data occurs.

line segment A geometric figure that represents the shortest path between two points, called the *endpoints* of the segment.

list price See *regular price*.

longitude The measure of an angle, whose vertex is the center of the earth, used to indicate the location of a place with reference to the prime meridian.

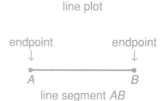

line plot

line segment *AB*

map scale The ratio of distances on a map or globe to the actual distances.

maximum The greatest value in a set of data.

mean An average of a set of numbers. To find the mean of a set of numbers, add the numbers and divide the sum by the number of numbers in the set.

median The middle value in a set of data, listed in order from smallest to largest (or largest to smallest).

minimum The smallest value in a set of data.

mode The value or category that occurs most often in a set of data.

multiplication fact The product of two numbers, each a number from 0 through 10.

nonconvex *See concave*.

number model A number sentence used to represent the relationship between quantities in a number story.

number sentence A sentence that is either true or false, made up of numerals, operation symbols (+, −, *, /), and relation symbols (=, <, >).

numerator In a whole divided into a number of equal parts, the number of equal parts being considered. In the fraction $\frac{a}{b}$, *a* is the numerator.

obtuse angle An angle that measures more than 90° and less than 180°.

octagon A polygon with eight sides.

octahedron A polyhedron with eight faces. (See *regular polyhedron*.)

open sentence A number sentence in which missing numbers are represented by letters or other symbols.

obtuse angle

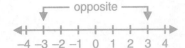
opposite

parallelogram

pentagon

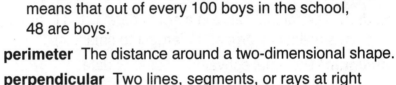
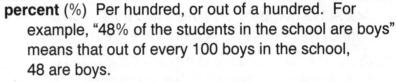
$\overleftrightarrow{CD}$ is perpendicular to $\overleftrightarrow{AB}$

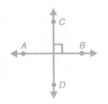
polygon with interior shaded

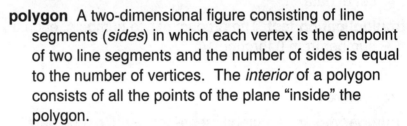
4 * 3 = 12
factors   product

quadrangle

opposite of a number On a number line, a number and its opposite are the same distance from zero. For example, the opposite of +3 is –3; the opposite of –5 is +5.

ordered pair Two numbers, given in a specific order, used to identify points on a coordinate grid. (For example, (2,3).)

parallel lines (segments, rays) Lines (segments, rays) that are the same distance apart and never meet, no matter how far they are extended.

parallelogram A quadrilateral in which pairs of opposite sides are parallel.

pentagon A polygon with five sides.

percent (%) Per hundred, or out of a hundred. For example, "48% of the students in the school are boys" means that out of every 100 boys in the school, 48 are boys.

perimeter The distance around a two-dimensional shape.

perpendicular Two lines, segments, or rays at right angles to each other.

polygon A two-dimensional figure consisting of line segments (*sides*) in which each vertex is the endpoint of two line segments and the number of sides is equal to the number of vertices. The *interior* of a polygon consists of all the points of the plane "inside" the polygon.

power of a number A number that can be expressed as the product of a number used as a factor two or more times. For example, 1000 (= 10 * 10 * 10) is the third power of 10 (10 to the third power). See *exponential notation*.

pre-image A picture or object before it is reflected through a transparent mirror.

product The result of multiplying two numbers, called *factors*. For example, in 4 * 3 = 12, 12 is the product.

quadrangle (quadrilateral) A polygon with four sides.

range The difference between the maximum and minimum in a set of data.

rate of discount The rate, usually given as a fraction or a percent, by which the *regular price* of an item on sale is reduced. For example, if an item whose regular price is $50, goes on sale for $40, the *discount* is $10 and the *rate of discount* is 20%.

rate of interest *See interest.*

ray A geometric figure that can be thought of as a line segment that extends in one direction without end.

ray *AB*

rectangle A parallelogram whose angles are all right angles.

rectangular coordinate grid A grid formed by two number lines that intersect at right angles at their 0 points.

rectangular coordinate grid

reflection A "flipping" motion of a picture or object so that its image is the opposite of the original *(the pre-image).*

reflex angle An angle that measures more than 180°.

reflex angle

regular polygon A convex polygon in which all sides are the same length and all angles are the same size.

regular polyhedron A polyhedron with faces that are all identical (the same size and shape). There are five regular polyhedrons:

regular hexagon

tetrahedron	4 faces, each formed by an equilateral triangle
cube	6 faces, each formed by a square
octahedron	8 faces, each formed by an equilateral triangle
dodecahedron	12 faces, each formed by a regular pentagon
icosahedron	20 faces, each formed by an equilateral triangle

tetrahedron   cube

regular price (list price) The price of an item without a discount.

rhombus A parallelogram whose sides are all the same length.

right angle An angle that measures 90°.

octahedron   dodecahedron

rotation A turn about a center point or axis.

rounding Changing a number between two numbers to the one it is closer to.

icosahedron

sale price The price of an item after a *discount* is subtracted from the *regular price.*

scale The ratio of a distance on a map, globe, or drawing to the actual distance.

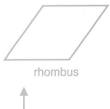
rhombus

scale drawing An accurate picture of an object that has each of its parts drawn according to the same scale.

right angle

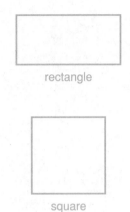
rectangle

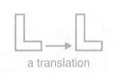
square

straight angle

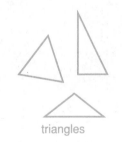
a translation

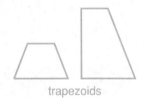
trapezoids

triangles

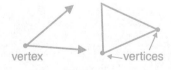
vertex   vertices

scientific notation A notational system in which a number is written as the product of a number between 1 and 10 and a power of 10.

side Any one of the line segments that make up a polygon.

solution of an open sentence The number used to replace the *variable* to make a true sentence.

square A rectangle whose sides are all the same length.

square (of a number) The product of a number multiplied by itself. For example, the square of 5 is 5 * 5, or 25.

square number A product of a whole number multiplied by itself. For example, 25 is a square number, because 25 = 5 * 5.

square unit A unit used in an area measurement.

straight angle An angle that measures 180°.

symmetric A picture or object that has at least one line of symmetry.

tally chart A table that displays each occurrence of a piece of data with a tally mark.

tetrahedron A polyhedron with four faces. (See *regular polyhedron.*)

translation (slide) The motion of an object or picture along a straight line.

trapezoid A quadrilateral with exactly one pair of parallel sides.

triangle A polygon with three sides and three angles.

turn A rotation.

turn-around facts Two multiplication facts whose factors and products are the same. (The factors are in a different order.)

two-dimensional shape A shape completely within a flat surface.

variable The letter or symbol that represents a missing number in an open sentence.

vertex The point at which the rays of an angle or two sides of a polygon meet.

vertices Plural of *vertex.*

volume The measure of the space inside a three-dimensional figure.

Bzzzzz...

Beetrice, the bee, wants to gather pollen from each flower and then return to her hive. Use your transparent mirror to help Beetrice fly around.

Activity Sheet 11 (front)

Build a Clown

Use the transparent mirror to put a hat on the clown's head. When the hat is where you want it, draw the hat. Do the same thing with the other missing parts to complete the clown picture. Color the picture and cut it out.

Name _____ Date _____ Time _____

Dart Game

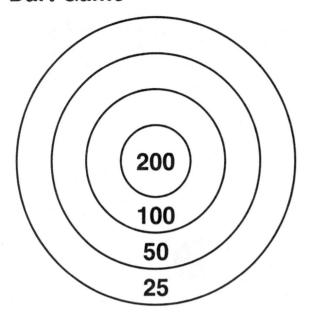

Scoreboard 1	
Player 1	**Player 2**

Scoreboard 2	
Player 1	**Player 2**

Scoreboard 3	
Player 1	**Player 2**

Use with Lesson 79.

Activity Sheet 12 (front)

Pocket-Billiard Game

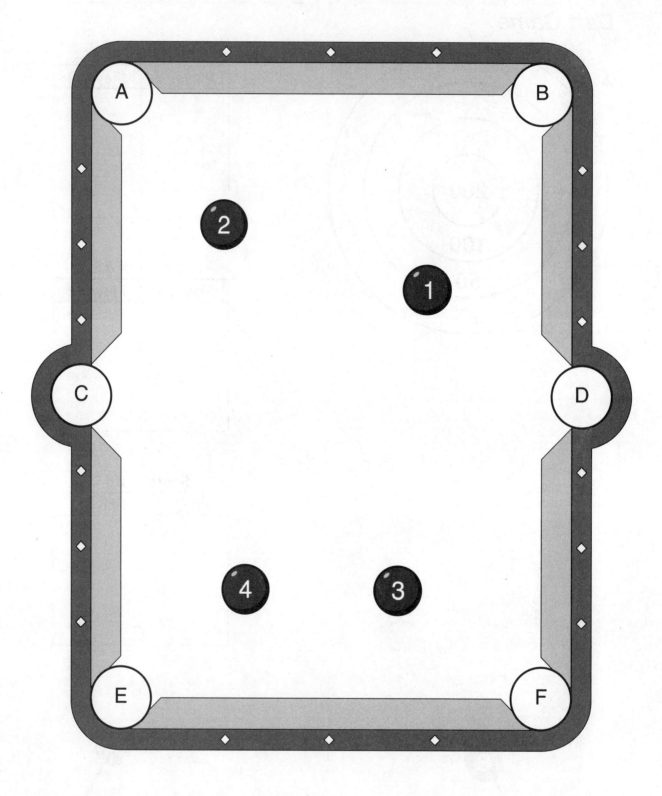

Names _____ Date _____ Time _____

_____

Reflections

1. Use the transparent mirror to draw the image of the head of the dog.

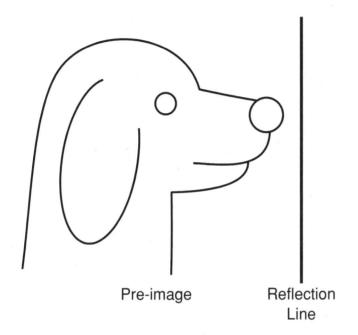

Pre-image   Reflection   Image
Line

2. Draw a picture on the left side of the line. Ask your partner to use the transparent mirror to draw the image of your picture.

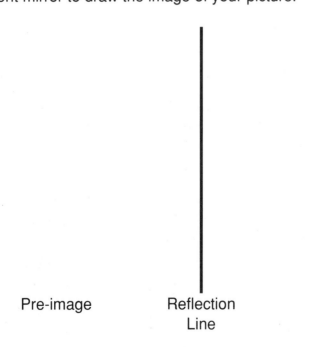

Pre-image   Reflection   Image
Line

Use with Lesson 80.

      Activity Sheet 13

Name _____ Date _____ Time _____

Half-Pictures

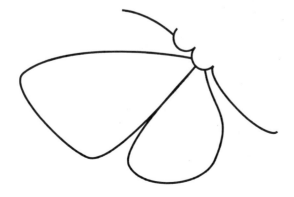

Activity Sheet 14

Symmetric Pictures

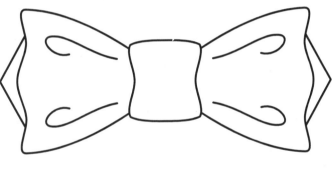

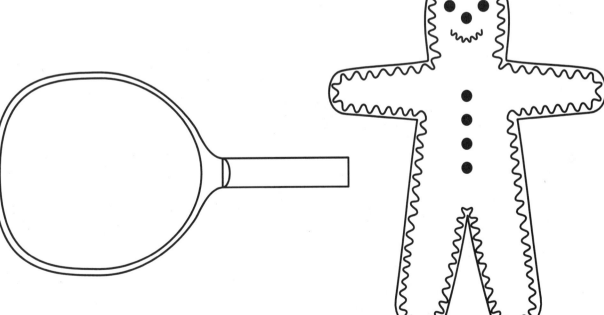

Polygons

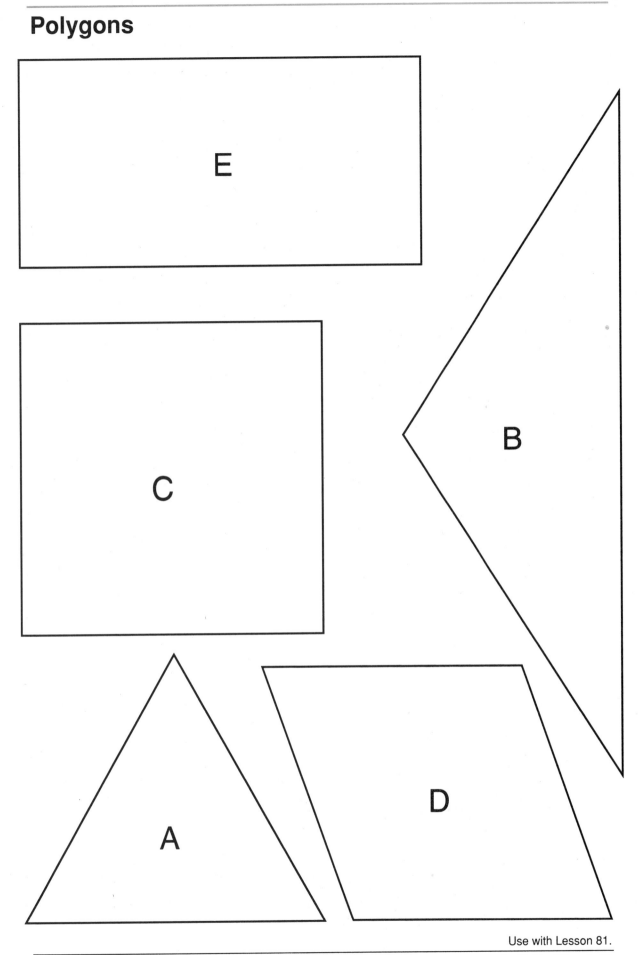

© 1995 Everyday Learning Corporation.

Activity Sheet 16

Polygons

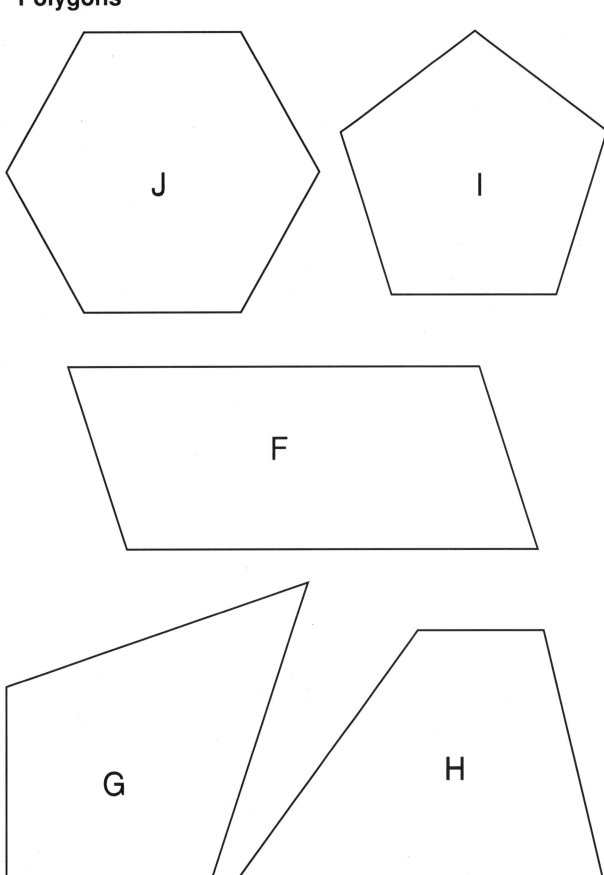

Activity Sheet 18

9-Patch Pattern Grid

Activity Sheet 19

Area of Parallelograms

Cut out parallelogram A. (Use the second parallelogram A if you make a mistake.)
Cut it into 2 pieces so that it can be made into a rectangle. Tape the rectangle on
page 269 in your journal.

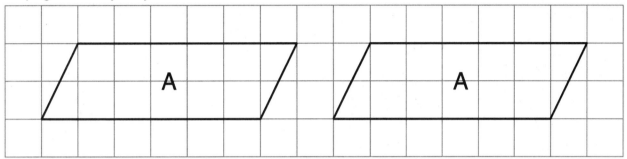

Do the same with parallelograms B, C, and D.

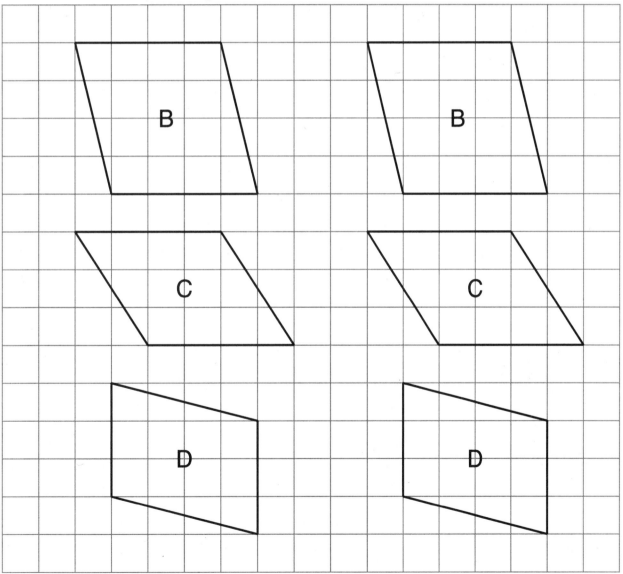

Area of Parallelograms

Area of Triangles

Cut out triangles A and B. Tape them together at the shaded corners to form a parallelogram. Tape the parallelogram in the space next to triangle A on page 275 in your journal.

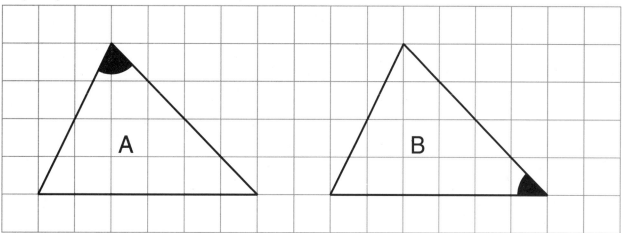

Do the same with the other 3 pairs of triangles.

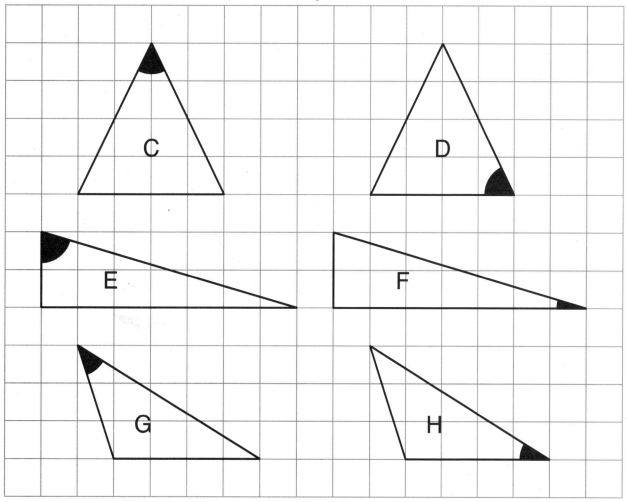

Activity Sheet 21

Quilt Patch

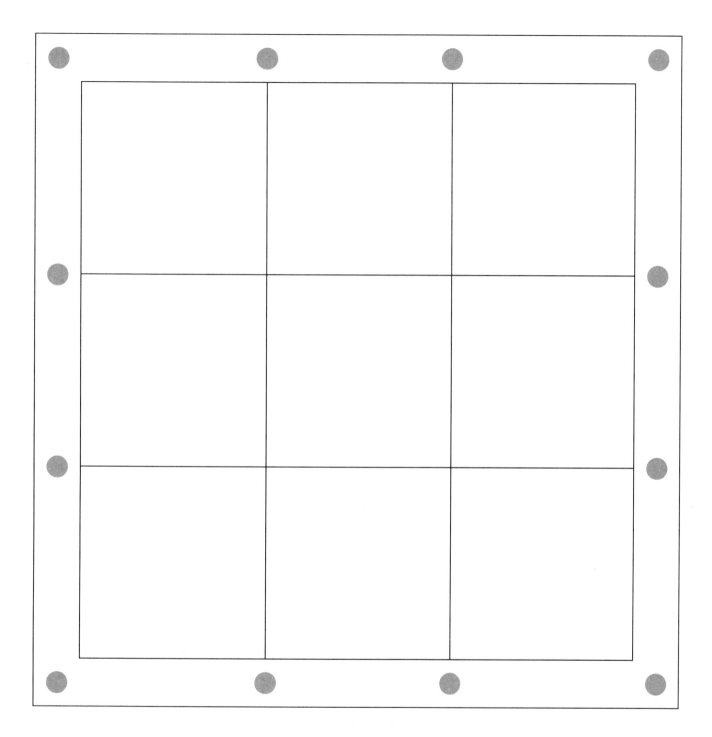

Use with Lesson 84.

Activity Sheet 22

Quilt Patch

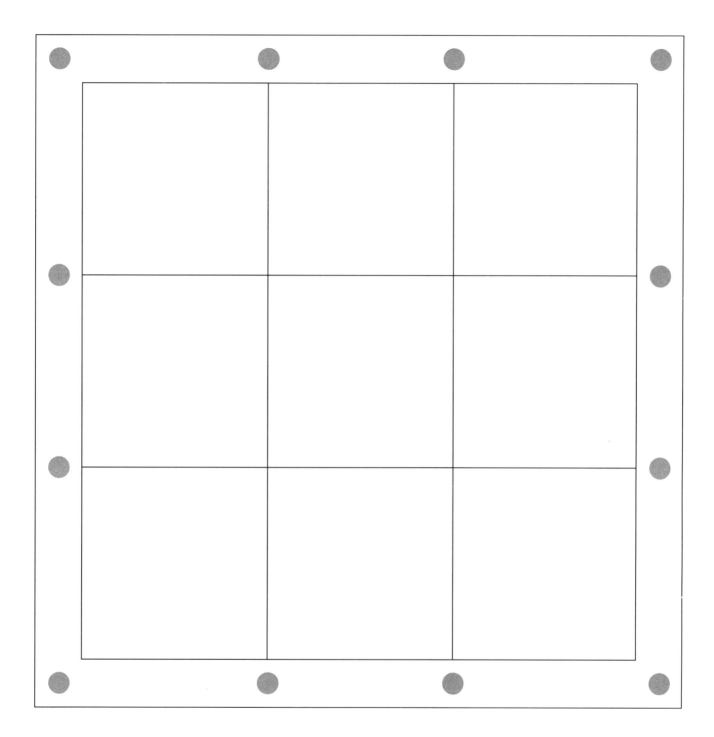

Quilt Patch

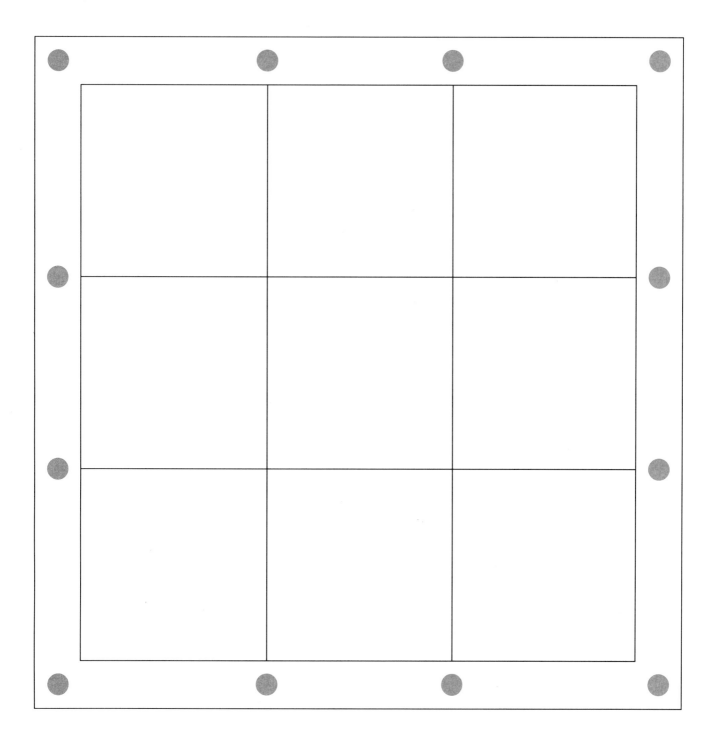

Use with Lesson 84.

Activity Sheet 24

Quilt-Pattern Shapes

Fraction/Percent Tiles

10%	20%	25%	30%
40%	50%	60%	70%
75%	80%	90%	100%
$\frac{1}{2}$	$\frac{1}{4}$	$\frac{3}{4}$	$\frac{1}{5}$
$\frac{2}{5}$	$\frac{3}{5}$	$\frac{4}{5}$	$\frac{1}{10}$
$\frac{3}{10}$	$\frac{7}{10}$	$\frac{9}{10}$	$\frac{2}{2}$

Use with Lesson 88.

%	%	%	%
%	%	%	%
%	%	%	%
$\dfrac{a}{b}$	$\dfrac{a}{b}$	$\dfrac{a}{b}$	$\dfrac{a}{b}$
$\dfrac{a}{b}$	$\dfrac{a}{b}$	$\dfrac{a}{b}$	$\dfrac{a}{b}$
$\dfrac{a}{b}$	$\dfrac{a}{b}$	$\dfrac{a}{b}$	$\dfrac{a}{b}$

Activity Sheet 26 (back)

PAR PORTION	
Calories	400
Protéines	35 g
Matières grasses	21 g
Glucides	20 g
Fibres	3 g
Fer	2 mg
Calcium	153 mg
Sodium	777 mg

Salade de poulet grillé à la thaï

Préparation : 15 minutes – **Marinage :** 12 heures
Cuisson : 12 minutes – **Quantité :** 4 portions

4	poitrines de poulet sans peau de 125 g chacune

Pour la vinaigrette :

2	oranges (jus)
2	limes (jus)
45 ml	(3 c. à soupe) de sauce soya
30 ml	(2 c. à soupe) de vinaigre de riz
30 ml	(2 c. à soupe) d'huile de sésame (non grillé)
15 ml	(1 c. à soupe) de gingembre haché
15 ml	(1 c. à soupe) d'ail haché
15 ml	(1 c. à soupe) de miel
	Piment fort au goût

Pour la salade :

12	mini-bok choys émincés
4	shiitakes
1	poivron rouge émincé
250 ml	(1 tasse) de fèves germées
45 ml	(3 c. à soupe) d'arachides rôties
45 ml	(3 c. à soupe) de coriandre émincée
30 ml	(2 c. à soupe) d'huile d'olive
—	

1. Mélanger les ingrédients de la vinaigrette et en verser la moitié dans un sac de plastique. Ajouter le poulet et laisser mariner de 12 à 24 heures au frais. Réserver le reste de la vinaigrette au frais.

2. Au moment de la cuisson, préchauffer le barbecue à puissance moyenne-élevée. Égoutter les poitrines et jeter la marinade.

3. Sur la grille chaude et huilée, saisir les poitrines 1 minute de chaque côté.

4. Régler le barbecue à puissance moyenne. Fermer le couvercle et cuire les poitrines de 6 à 8 minutes de chaque côté, jusqu'à ce que l'intérieur de la chair ait perdu sa teinte rosée. Émincer le poulet.

5. Verser la vinaigrette réservée dans un saladier. Ajouter les ingrédients de la salade et mélanger. Répartir dans les assiettes. Garnir de poulet.

—

PAR PORTION	
Calories	222
Protéines	10 g
Matières grasses	15 g
Glucides	12 g
Fibres	2,6 g
Fer	2 mg
Calcium	65 mg
Sodium	82 mg

Crevettes grillées
et courgettes marinées

Préparation : 15 minutes — **Trempage :** 30 minutes — **Cuisson :** 4 minutes — **Quantité :** 4 portions

60 ml	(¼ de tasse) d'huile d'olive
15 ml	(1 c. à soupe) de vinaigre de riz
15 ml	(1 c. à soupe) de coriandre hachée
15 ml	(1 c. à soupe) de sucre
5 ml	(1 c. à thé) d'ail haché
5 ml	(1 c. à thé) de piments forts hachés
2	oignons verts émincés
2	limes (jus et zeste)
4	courgettes
12	crevettes moyennes (calibre 31/40), crues et décortiquées

—

1. Faire tremper 12 mini-brochettes de bois 30 minutes dans l'eau.

2. Préparer la marinade en mélangeant tous les ingrédients, à l'exception des courgettes et des crevettes. Diviser la préparation en deux : une moitié servira à badigeonner et l'autre, comme sauce d'accompagnement.

3. Couper les courgettes en fines tranches sur la longueur.

4. Préchauffer le barbecue à puissance moyenne.

5. Préparer les mini-brochettes en piquant une crevette sur chacune d'elles. À l'aide d'un pinceau, badigeonner les courgettes et les crevettes avec la moitié de la marinade.

6. Sur la grille chaude et huilée du barbecue, griller les crevettes et les tranches de courgettes de 2 à 3 minutes de chaque côté. Servir avec le reste de la marinade.

—

Filets de tilapia
au pesto et citron

Préparation : 15 minutes — **Marinage :** 1 heure (facultatif) — **Cuisson :** 8 minutes — **Quantité :** 4 portions

30 ml	(2 c. à soupe) de pesto
15 ml	(1 c. à soupe) de zestes de citron
15 ml	(1 c. à soupe) de câpres hachées
30 ml	(2 c. à soupe) de ciboulette hachée
15 ml	(1 c. à soupe) d'huile d'olive
4	filets de tilapia
—	

1. Préchauffer le barbecue à puissance moyenne-élevée.

2. Dans un plat creux, mélanger le pesto avec les zestes de citron, les câpres, la ciboulette et l'huile. Déposer les filets de tilapia dans le plat et retourner afin de les enrober de la préparation. Si désiré, laisser mariner 1 heure au frais.

3. Sur la grille chaude et huilée du barbecue, cuire les filets de 4 à 5 minutes de chaque côté.

—

Index des recettes